WK275

GUY ELLIS
WK275

THE RESTORATION AND PRESERVATION OF THE LAST
SUPERMARINE SWIFT F4

GRUB STREET
LONDON

Published by
GRUB STREET
4 Rainham Close
London SW11 6SS

Copyright © Grub Street 2017
Copyright text © Guy Ellis 2017

A CIP record for this title is
available from the British Library

ISBN-13: 978-1-910690-50-5

Design by Daniele Roa

Printed and bound by Finidr,
Czech Republic

Contents

ACKNOWLEDGEMENTS

It was a sunny day in April 2017 when I knocked on a door in Herefordshire. It was opened by a couple who were naturally wary of a complete stranger who was asking questions about an old aircraft. It took a few minutes before mutual interest got the conversation going and it was agreed that I could return in a couple of weeks. When I did, I was presented with the most amazing hospitality. The couple had gathered together and retrieved from forty years' storage all the items they had, relevant to that aircraft and we sat down to a wonderful few hours of old documents, newspaper cuttings, photographs and reminiscences. That couple were Derick and Ann Sheppard whose family had displayed WK275 outside their business in rural Herefordshire for forty-four years. The generosity of spirit and abiding interest in an important part of aviation history, epitomised by the Sheppards, is the mainstay of this book. There are many people acknowledged below, each of whom was generous with their time, knowledge, and artefacts.

My thanks to Tim Wood who owns WK275 and thought of the idea and Chris Wilson, of Jet Art Aviation who restored WK275. Both have given me hours of time over email, the phone and in person. Chris has provided all the images of the restoration of the aircraft, accompanied by very patient explanations and corrections to the text. I am indebted to him and have enjoyed our time working together.

I was lucky enough to talk to several men who had served with various marks of the Swift and gave freely of their time, writing, and talking about their experiences, some of whom have been quoted extensively. It was a privilege to have the photographs and insights from Sandy Burns, Edward Duke, Barry Flahey, Alan Middleton, Ron Mortley via his daughter Jill Warby, Roy Rimington, John Sawyer, Eric Sharp and Nigel Walpole. The latter has written several books, one of which *Swift Justice* I would consider to be the definitive work on the Vickers Supermarine Swift.

Several organisations and the people working there, many volunteers, answered my calls and messages and helped direct me to the right place or person and contributed to this endeavour. Lee Barton, Air Force Historical Branch (RAF) photo archivist gave me such clear and comprehensive assistance. Clive Chapman of QinetiQ put me in touch with Norman Parker and steered me through the A&AEE, Andrew Costerton of Flight Global kindly took my repeated copyright queries and of course the fabulous Flight Global archive is a wonderful resource for a view of the contemporary. Trevor Friend of BAE Systems was often a friendly voice on the end of a phone or email with quiet guidance on that tricky subject copyright. David Gash of Solent Sky Museum spent time working through their archives for me and providing what was relevant. David Holden, a local South Marston historian, ex-Vickers and who gives talks on that company, gave his insights and background to life where the Swifts were built. He put me in touch with Ann Marie Murphy of the Highworth Historical Society, who kindly provided me with images from South Marston. Phil Marris from www.ourhatfield.org.uk assisted with finding ex-de Havilland employees. Many other organisations, not mentioned, were contacted and sometimes when it was established they had nothing on the Swift they often gave me ideas as to where I could go next.

The following museums allowed the use of their images and provided background data: Pete Pitman from Tangmere Military Aviation Museum, Mike Smith of Newark Air Museum, and Ron Fulton of the Boscombe Down Aviation Collection.

Naturally the service organisations and websites were an early port of call. Mick Ryan of www.rafjever.org runs an unbelievably good site with so much information, which is thoroughly indexed and cross referenced. Of course, this site was invaluable and Mick's help despite illness is hugely appreciated. Jez Holmes of II (AC) Squadron Association, put out an appeal to all members on their site. While Squadron Leader Andy Smith, executive officer and Flight Lieutenant Michael Frankel of No. 56 (Reserve) Squadron trawled through their archives, and along with Brain Spurway of 81st Entry RAF Halton put out requests for members to share their memories. From the Boulton Paul Association, Les Whitehouse provided some wonderful images and Jack Holmes a comprehensive piece on the modification of the dog-toothed wing.

For projects of this nature photographs are paramount and I have relied on the massive generosity of the photographers listed below who have made a very significant contribution to this publication. Peter Arnold, world renowned Spitfire specialist for once again helping, Faustine Carrera of Fédération Aéronautique Internationale, Peter Clarke for his help for the fourth time, Jerry Hughes for freely lending his images, Jacques Schelfaut and Johan Engels from www.thunderstreaks.com, Francis Wallace, who documented in photographs WK275 at Leominster, Chris Wilson of Jet Art Aviation, Mark Worthington of A. M. Frames, Neil Corbett of thetartanterror.blogspot.co.uk and Tony Hawes. Thank you.

There are a special set of people who do not fit into any of the above groups. These are what I term fellow travellers or enthusiasts. I spent a wonderful afternoon with Boscombe Down historian Norman Parker, whose memory of the details was astounding. David Key the archivist at Hursely Park for his fellowship chats, Denis Kay who first purchased WK275 for his insights into a long-gone time of military surplus buying. Mike and David Thorne, the sons of Air Commodore Peter Thorne OBE AFC (senior test pilot – Swift) a highly acclaimed test pilot, for their enthusiasm for the project and the memories of their father's work. Gary Eason whom I enjoyed working with to develop the front cover and Nathan Decker whose 'biographical' data on several 'Forgotten Jets' http://www.millionmonkeytheater.com/ForgottenJets.html, is a great kick-off point. Finally, Robert Forsyth for his help and guidance in the early days of the project.

My apologies to anyone whom I have inadvertently omitted because of my careless recording or to whom I had a fleeting interaction as I was guided to those above; there were many who helped.

I have made every effort to establish the correct ownership of materials used and to obtain permission to use, or arranged a licence and acknowledge sources of the items used. If however, I have made an error it is rather through ignorance than design for which I apologise as copyright is a very important concept that I take seriously.

Guy Ellis
2017

FOREWORD

Military aircraft watchers in the early 1950s took great interest in the race between the Supermarine Swift and the Hawker Hunter to become the next generation air defence fighter, and those of us who flew variants of both aircraft would not challenge the decision to declare the Hunter the winner in that role. However, we should not deny Supermarine credit for pressing on with an F4, WK275, its 'definitive fighter', and for its continued ingenuity, innovation and determination which led to the FR5, arguably the best low-level, short-range armed reconnaissance fighter in NATO at the time, and the F7, a useful missile trials fighter.

Where possible, the F4 profited from all the lessons learned from its predecessors, while adding the innovative 'slab' tail, and it was an F4 – WK198 – which broke the world airspeed record, in September 1953, with Mike Lithgow at the controls. Sadly, after exhaustive tests on WK275, at the Aeroplane and Armament Experimental Establishment (A&AEE), the highly respected RAF test pilot, Peter Thorne, who flew all versions of the aircraft, could not recommend its employment by the RAF in the pure fighter role. WK275, the only F4 to survive complete, languished outside Sheppards Store, Leominster, for many years, gradually deteriorating, until its rescue in 2012.

In this book, Guy Ellis treats us to a comprehensive reminder of the torturous evolution of the Swift family, with WK275 a unique icon of British endeavour in the 1950s. In his excellent resumé on its more recent life, he pays proper tribute to Tim Wood for his most generous contribution to our aviation heritage and to Chris Wilson and his Jet Art Aviation team for their meticulous restoration. *WK275 – The Restoration and Preservation of the Last Supermarine Swift F4* is a valuable addition to that family's history.

Group Captain Nigel J. R. Walpole
OBE BA FRAeS RAF (Ret'd)

PREFACE

This book celebrates the restoration of WK275, a rare but relatively well known airframe. In doing so the technical and political environment in which it was created is explored, along with the development of its immediate predecessors. Production of the F4 ran to only eight airframes but these represent a significant step up from the first three versions and bridge to those that followed. The late 1940s through to the early 1960s was a period of intense discovery in the aviation world. Across the globe aeronautical engineers were learning about aerodynamics at high speed, metallurgists were creating new materials and understanding how these and older materials interacted, while mechanical engineers were building higher performing engines and pilots were adapting their skills to their new tools.

Changes required to the tried and tested Second World War methods were dramatic and sudden. Britain was war weary and struggling to restore its battered economy within which dynamic scientific encounters were taking place at a rapid rate. The Allied countries scrambled to benefit from what they found in the defeated German world of science and to incorporate this knowledge to solve problems they had encountered moving into the jet age.

The significant advantage of the early development of the jet engine was carelessly cast aside by the British aviation world, through lack of understanding, petty jealousies, and fear of failure. An unknown pilot scientist Frank Whittle understood that an entirely new type of propulsion system was required to be able to reach the thinner air found at altitude and reach speeds unachievable with a piston engine and propeller. His thesis received 100% but when he presented it to the Air Ministry in 1929, their reviewing scientist A. A. Griffith rejected the concept and Whittle was left to go it alone. Having no money, he was forced to let the patent lapse and it was very quickly picked up by German diplomats in London.

Eventually Whittle managed to raise the funds and some government interest and on 15 May 1941 the Gloster E28/39, powered by the Power Jets W1 engine flew for the first time with test pilot Gerry Sayer at the controls. This was the most dramatic change in aviation since the Wright brothers first flight. Although the German Heinkel He 178 was the first jet to fly, it was from the Whittle jet engine that all jet aircraft are descended. Wartime secrecy and the potential to develop a weapon that could vanquish the Nazis meant a momentous occasion went unannounced and virtually unrecorded.

This event heralded an age of fantastic advancement in engineering. Exploration into realms and concepts never reached before and the extreme bravery of those that built and flew the aircraft, were all part of what we take for granted today. Manufacturers such as Supermarine risked their existence on reaching beyond the known and toward creating an advantage for themselves and for the country. The Swift achieved several firsts, at one stage it outshone its great rival the Hawker Hunter and in its later form it was loved by its pilots, if not so much by its ground crew.

It suffered from being right at the forefront of the fast jet revolution. The airframe was designed to take the more primitive centrifugal turbojet rather than the slimmer more advanced axial motor, which was not quite ready. When it was then fitted with an axial unit, there were neither the funds nor time to undertake a re-design. Everything about the aerodynamics was experimental, learnt as the designers went along. As there were no research and development funds, a viable product had to be produced, with the effect that everything was rushed and the complexities of flight at high speed and height were discovered in the air.

The Swift is mostly written up as a complete failure, one of the disasters of British aviation, but the story is not that simple. It was unquestionably plagued with problems, but the context in which these occurred must be examined. It was a pioneer, the first of the British swept-wing fighters, developed with minimal funding and originally designed as an experimental vehicle. It was a changing political environment that forced its operational deployment before the experiment was complete. Where there were two prototypes of the Swift, there were ten times that number of Hawker Hunter prototypes, and there was a significant three-year gap between the first flight of a Swift and that of a Hunter. Significant in that technology was moving so quickly that progress overtook design and many of the early 1950s jets became obsolete within an extraordinary short time. Much of what was introduced to the Royal Air Force for the first time was through the Swift, such as the swept-wing, afterburners, missile armament, a dog-toothed wing and the variable incidence tail plane. These were perfected later and can be seen in use in today's military and commercial aircraft.

The need for speed

SPEED GIVES US an advantage. It is vital for both attack and survival in combat, it provides that one step ahead essential in commerce, and makes heroes of the fastest athletes. Forward speed is all about thrust. It is a mechanical process where the propulsion mechanism is in physical contact with the medium in which the thrust occurs, for instance air, water, or land. An aero engine takes air and accelerates it rearwards which generates thrust in the opposite direction. It follows the principle of Sir Isaac Newton's Third Law of Motion, for every action, there is an equal and opposite reaction. Much like an inflated balloon that is released and shoots off in a crazy uncontrolled flight, in the opposite direction to the outflow of air. It is the effect of thrust that propels aircraft forward and overcomes the forces of drag holding it back. It is these two, thrust and drag, which impose a limit on the achievable top speed.

A piston engine does not produce thrust, rather it is used to spin a propeller which creates thrust via the difference in the air pressure between the front and the back of the propeller. To get the most out of the power of the engine the propeller needs to efficiently convert this energy into thrust. Ever since man's first flight, propellers have been under development. The aerofoil shape, variable pitch, contra rotating and multi blades have all been introduced to reduce drag, increase lift, and convert power to thrust.

Every manufacturer was producing increasingly powerful engines which combined with continually evolving more efficient propellers, created added thrust and faster aircraft. These engines became heavier, more complex to build and to maintain, but were still limited to the subsonic realm. The Spitfire Mk1a's Merlin motor produced 1,030 hp and a top speed of 367 mph (582 km/h), while the last 2,120 hp Griffon-powered F24 could reach 454 mph (731 km/h).

Piston-engine aircraft were at their peak when the first operational jet-powered aircraft came into service. Jet engines take in air, heat it, compress it and then it is released through the exhaust, where the air expands and accelerates, exerting more force forward than rearwards. Propeller power cannot accelerate air to the same extent. A propeller needs to rotate at impossibly high speeds to create the same thrust. The problem is that at top speed the tips of the blades reach supersonic speeds and the resulting Mach shocks, accompanied by severe buffeting, create a significant increase in drag. Effectively they reach the limit of their efficiency. The larger frontal area of the engines and the propellers of piston aircraft amplified drag, whereas jet aircraft are far more streamlined and their air intakes aerodynamically optimised.

First flown in May 1941 the Gloster E28/39 produced 850 lbs of thrust and had a top speed of 338 mph (544 km/h). Within ten months thrust had been increased to 1,000 lbs and the speed to 466 mph (750 km/h), faster than any piston-powered fighter in service at the time.

Although the need to identify and develop new metals and methods to withstand high temperatures and pressures hampered jet engine development, it was a relatively simple construction and so did not require heavy industrial equipment for manufacture. It cost less than the large developed piston engines, but as it was new technology there was a great deal to learn and overcome. The early jet engines were unreliable and proved to be very thirsty, limiting their range and effectiveness. As knowledge was gained and new materials and techniques emerged, reliability improved but through the early years fuel consumption and flight duration continued to be a concern.

Jet power and the promise of previously unattainable speeds increased the pressure from the military to take full advantage of the opportunities presented and competition to stay ahead was extremely fierce. The design techniques and manufacturing methods that had served Great Britain so well during the war were no longer relevant.

The location of the jet engine, coupled with the need for a short exhaust to take full advantage of the thrust and the attainable speeds, changed the aerodynamic forces. Barely understood characteristics of flight at heights and conditions never experienced before made this a golden era of discovery, bravery, and brilliance.

Cautiously designers fitted the radical new fuselage shapes with straight wings with reduced thickness ratios, the known way of reducing or pushing back the point at which Mach was reached across the wing. In the United Kingdom, the swept-wing advantage was known but its benefit over the straight laminar-flow wing was unclear. With little government support or other funding British industry adopted the low-cost option of adapting current models. Swept-wings increase the efficiency of the wing itself and combined with an optimum thickness and strength as well as the ability to carry weapons and fuel, all contributed to the change in designs which made the jet a very different and faster aircraft.

Other innovations were the differing air intake designs created to force as much air as possible into the engine with minimal air flow disruption. The all-moving tail was fashioned to provide pilots with control as they crossed through the transonic zone and into the supersonic realm and powered controls provided the feel of positive input to aileron management. In the never-ending chase for increased speed the after burner was invented to further heat the exhaust gases and create even more thrust.

The early jets benefited from the rapid developments that took place in the late 1940s through to the mid 1960s, but they were not capable of sustained supersonic speeds. They were very advanced subsonic aircraft that were capable, in dives and good conditions, to attain supersonic flight for short durations.

A side effect of this dramatic change in the aviation industry was that the aircraft became more complex, larger, and a great deal more expensive. Longer development times were required as new problems arose and solutions had to be devised. Along with these factors, the greater speed and robustness of the modern jet fighter over its piston forebears saw a reduction in the numbers produced and in most cases long years of service.

Compressibility

A fundamental physical limitation of the race for increased speed and the desire to make optimum use of the new power source was the concept of compressibility. As a boat moves through water it pushes a bow wave that must 'move' out of the way to allow the boat's passage. The faster the boat travels the larger the bow wave and the disturbance of water around the boat that we all know as the wake. Something similar occurs as an aircraft moves through the air.

If the speed is below 250 mph (402 km/h) the density of air ahead and around the aircraft remains largely unchanged. As the speed increases the air ahead of the aircraft becomes increasingly compressed, with resultant airflow changes across the airframe. The density of the air changes, which alters the aerodynamic forces of lift and drag that keep the aircraft aloft.

As the aircraft approaches supersonic speed, aerodynamic drag increases, which typically leads to a high-speed stall at the wingtip and an increased flow downwards over the tail plane. When aircraft in the Second World War were achieving very high speeds, the air flow changes and difficulty of control were perceived as a barrier to being able to attain any greater acceleration.

In popular idiom, this is known as 'breaking the sound barrier'. The speed of sound is measured as the ratio of the speed of the aircraft or the speed of the gas (air) to the speed of sound in the gas. The Mach measurement was named after the Austrian physicist Ernst Mach who in the 19th century specialised in studying shock waves.

Mach 1 is the speed of sound which in dry conditions at sea level and at a temperature of 20 °C (68 °F), is reached at a speed of 343 metres per second, which works out as about 767 mph (1,234 km/h). A decrease in temperature, such as that experienced at altitude decreases the speed needed to 'break the barrier'. For example, at 20,000 feet (6,096 metres) the speed of sound is 600 mph (1,063 km/h).

To be able to increase aircraft speeds and take advantage of the extra power provided by jet engines it was necessary to find a way of controlling the effects of the transition into the supersonic. The application of a swept-wing delayed the onset of transonic drag, increasing the wing speed which allowed the aircraft to travel at far higher transonic and supersonic speeds for the same energy expended by straight-wing planes at lower subsonic speeds.

Swept-wings had been flown before the First World War when John Dunne designed and built a series of tailless flying wing reconnaissance biplane gliders and then powered craft. Following medical discharge from the Wiltshire Regiment, Dunne embarked on aeronautical research with the specific interest in designing a safe aeroplane with integral aerodynamic stability. The swept plan

This flying wing is a replica constructed of mahogany, brass, fabric, and nitrate by Barry MacKeracher and represents a Canadian military observation aircraft known as the Burgess-Dunne. Designed by the English engineer John William Dunne (1875–1949) and built by the American boat and aircraft building company Burgess, which merged with Curtiss Aeroplane and Motor Company in 1916. It is on display at the National Air Force Museum of Canada.
(Brad Denoon, National Air Force Museum of Canada)

form provided longitudinal stability and would self-correct when gusts of wind caused a pitching motion. Many designers followed Dunne but the tailless self-stabilising aircraft lacked the manoeuvrability to be militarily useful, until that is the advent of the jet engine and the need to 'break the sound barrier'.

At the Volta Congress on High Speeds in Aviation conference held in Rome in 1935, German Adolf Busemann presented a paper on supersonic airflow, proposing that the use of swept-wings would enable supersonic flight. At the time aircraft speeds were not much more than 300 mph (483 km/h) and therefore the concept was purely an academic construct. Busemann, along with other German aeronautical engineers continued to work on the concept and by the end of the war they were testing numerous transonic and supersonic aircraft and missile designs. Around the same time an American aerodynamicist at the Langley Memorial Aeronautical Laboratory, Robert Jones, had independently documented the benefits of minimising drag by sweeping the wing behind the Mach cone or pressure wave generated at supersonic speed.

The capture and detailed examination of the German experiments and the employment of German scientists confirmed Robert Jones' concept, which at the time, had been largely rejected by American academics. Although the swept-wing enabled the attainment of

The North American F-86F Sabre and Mikoyan-Gurevich MiG-15 could not be matched by the British aviation industry in the 1950s. The Sabre c/n 191-708, 12834 / FU-834 'Jolley Roger' (NX186AM), served in the USAF with serial 52-5012 and in the Argentinian air force as C-127. Currently in the markings of the 335th Fighter-Interceptor Squadron, part of the 4th Fighter-Interceptor Wing and painted as the aircraft used by Captain Clifford D. Jolley in the Korean War, with which he scored seven victories. The MiG c/n 91051, 1051 (NX87CN) is a Russian-manufactured airframe that served with the Chinese air force as '83277' and is seen here in North Korean air force markings. Both airworthy aircraft are held at the Planes of Fame Museum, Chino, California, USA. (*Linda Bell*)

supersonic speeds, there were significant handling issues around stability and control at all speeds which had to be overcome.

The upward or dihedral angle of the wing from the horizontal affects the lateral stability resulting in a 'Dutch roll'. When a swept-wing aircraft yaws, for instance changes direction to the right in a flat manner, the left wing's angle becomes less swept to the oncoming air and develops more lift, causing a roll to the right. Corrective action then creates the opposite conditions and the aircraft rolls to the left. Yaw dampers are required which have sensors that provide control inputs to the rudder to reduce the roll effect.

In a straight-winged aircraft when lift is lost in a stall condition this change occurs across the whole length of the wing and the nose tends to drop. With the early jets the opposite condition occurred at both low and high speeds. When the wing begins to stall, lift is first lost at the wingtips and then progresses inward which shifts the lift forces forward, resulting in a nose pitch up attitude. Often the stall is not uniform with the result of an increased loss of lift on one wing and a roll would be induced. Additionally, as the ailerons were located on the outer wings they would become ineffective at a point when the pilot desperately required some input to correct a rapidly deteriorating situation. Pitch up would rob a military pilot of the ability to engage an enemy and could result in airframe damage and ultimately in mid-air disintegration.

Probably the three most recognised fighters of the era were the North American Sabre F-86, the Mikoyan-Gurevich MiG-15 and the Hawker Hunter, were all susceptible to the adverse effects of transonic flight. The Sabre first flew in October 1947 and over the years became as famous and well renowned as the wartime P-51 Mustang from the same manufacturer. Built in three countries in thirty-two variants it served in twenty-eight air forces, with the last retired by Argentina in 1986. The RAF, frustrated by the lack of availability of a British-built swept-wing fighter and concerned their straight-winged Meteors and Vampires were no threat to the MiG-15-equipped Warsaw PACT air forces, purchased three Canadair Sabre Mk2 and 427 Mk4s in October 1952.

However, all was not perfect. *Flight International* noted in their 2 January 1964 issue that a characteristic of the F-86 was 'if the tip loss is asymmetric (occurring on one wing before the other) the aircraft will experience wing dropping or "roll off", possibly in combination with an uncontrolled yawing manoeuvre'. Dr Hallion quotes that Michael Collins, in his autobiography *Carrying the Fire: An Astronaut's Journey* remembered his introduction to the F-86 noting 'in the eleven weeks I was there (Nellis Air Force Base), twenty-two people were killed. In retrospect, it seems preposterous to endure such casualty rates without help from the enemy, but at the time the risk appeared perfectly acceptable.'

Swept-wing fighters of the 1950s era from left to right: Supermarine Swift FR5, Hawker Hunter F4 and Canadair Sabre F4. The FR5, XD910/B was delivered in January 1956 to II (AC) Squadron. It crashed on 22 August 1957 near Aachen, West Germany killing the pilot Flight Lieutenant Richard Greenhalgh. Hunter F4, XF309 was delivered in January 1956 and written off by the air force of Zimbabwe in July 1982. Sabre F4 was delivered in June 1953 and damaged beyond repair in December 1958. *(Ron Mortley)*

It was no different with the Sabre's arch rival the MiG-15. Fitted with a fixed tail and halfway down the fin, the horizontal tail surfaces, the Soviet fighter was prone to loss of tail surface control when air flow was blanked off by the main planes. The consequential severe pitch up limited combat manoeuvrability and many examples were lost because of an aerodynamic stall and subsequent flat irrecoverable spin. Poor quality control meant that the two wings were never the same and as an aircraft approached Mach 1 the pilot would experience uncontrollable rolling. Despite its problems, it served in forty-three air forces, was built in three countries and production ran to 18,000 airframes compared to the 9,860 Sabres and only 1,972 Hawker Hunters.

Following early design work from 1948, the first Hunter prototype flew in July 1951. By 1953 the first production F1s became available and twenty-two were earmarked as development airframes. Early on problems emerged. Use of airbrakes resulted in pitch down attitude, firing the cannon at height caused the engine to flame out and the spent cartridges caused severe damage to the underside of the fuselage. The engines suffered from surging and cutting out, and at low speed, without powered controls the Hunter was liable to enter a Dutch roll, while at altitude and toward the supersonic range the nose would pitch up. It would be correct to say that the first two marks of the Hunter were not service ready and it was only from the Mk6 onward that Hawker's fighter came into its own.

All the manufacturers focused on addressing the effects of compressibility. Major design changes were undertaken and new aerodynamic laws established. Some adopted full span leading edge flaps to address the pitch up tendency, others experimented with a slab tail fin, with and without a variable tail plane. Wing fences were used to induce a stall toward the centre of the wing and delay its progression outwards and so extend the time that the ailerons were effective, giving the pilot more time to react and recover.

A new development was the introduction of a saw-tooth leading edge to the wing which served to improve lift at low speeds and reduce drag at high speeds. Introduced on high swept-wings the leading-edge extension works by creating a vortex behind it and in a similar way to a wing fence prevents the separated airflow from moving outboard at high angle of attack. This along with the all-moving horizontal tail surfaces have become standard in both modern military and commercial aircraft.

CHAPTER 2

Super priority

WHEN THE CONSERVATIVE PARTY won the general election on 25 October 1951, 77-year-old Winston Churchill became prime minister for the second time. At the time wartime rationing was still in place and over half the population lived in rented accommodation, which was often cramped, unheated and dreary.

The Royal Air Force and Royal Navy were second only in size to the equivalent United States forces. However, many of the aircraft were obsolete but jet-powered Gloster Meteors and de Havilland Vampires signified the future and had impressed the world's piston-driven air arms. Britain led the way in jet technology but despite the manufacturers developing new ideas and products, the British aviation industry fell behind in the race for aeronautical leadership.

Government support had not been forthcoming and the plan was to only begin to re-equip the air force from 1957. The sudden outbreak of war on the Korean peninsula created an urgent need to bring into service second-generation jet aircraft. It was patently clear that the Russian-built MiG-15 was faster and more manoeuvrable than the RAF's premier fighter, the Meteor.

Britain did not have the financial resources to be able to fund large-scale development projects. The defence budget was £1,462 million and of that £600 million was earmarked to produce current equipment. Churchill's government aimed to prevent an increase in defence spending, but at the same time encourage the all-important export market, which would 'not only contribute to the security of the free world, but will also help to maintain the war potential of British industry.'[1]

[1] Hansard 04 December 1952 vol 508 cc1775-82.

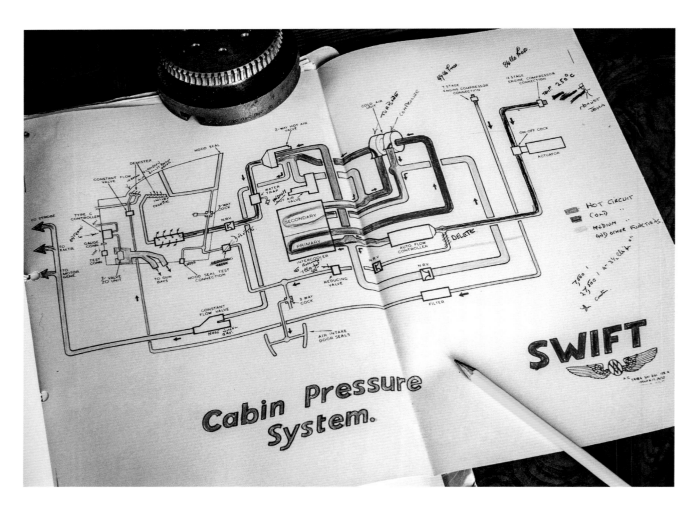

A fold-out from a Swift engineering manual laid out in a workshop with details of the Swift's cabin pressure system. (Tim Wood)

Plans to accelerate a rearmament programme were announced in London on 26 March 1952 by Mr F. C. Musgrave, CB, deputy secretary, Ministry of Supply. Known as the 'super priorities scheme', it was created to ensure that contractors would have all the necessary resources to deliver the government plan. It was clear that the scheme was focused on development rather than production, as the Hawker Sea Hawk and de Havilland Venom, due to enter service in 1952, had not been included.

A result of the war was that manufacturers had too many design offices and fragmented factories to be efficient or coherent. In general, they were understaffed, under-funded and stretched far too wide, working on too many, often competing civilian and military projects. The focus was on the new technology, and the desperate need to sign a government contract to be able to survive, with the result that the export market was almost an after-thought.

A list of super-priority aviation projects was issued. The first step in the plan was to cut costs, by delivering over a longer period and to reduce the number of types being produced and so facilitate the rapid introduction of new generation military jet aircraft. Defence spending depended on the development of the economy and a healthy balance of payments. The emphasis on the super priority aircraft meant that the government had to reduce orders for current equipment, despite their worthwhile capabilities, purely to enable the introduction of more modern types.

On the super priority list were the Hawker Hunter, Supermarine Swift, English Electric Canberra, Vickers Valiant, Fairey Gannet and the de Havilland DH110 (Sea Vixen) or Gloster GA5 (Javelin). Only the Canberra was in service and achieving enviable export orders. Its success as a medium bomber and its versatility meant that plans to develop a light bomber were terminated. Included was the development and supply of ammunition for the new aircraft, equipment for the radar chain, Centurion tanks, missiles, and their related guidance systems. To allay fears of severe disruption to wider production, Parliament was advised that the expected output of the priorities list only represented two and a half per cent of the metal-based engineering industrial sector.

The minister of Supply, Mr Duncan Sandys, stated that main and subcontractors could, when necessary, expedite deliveries by preceding the reference contract number with the words 'super priority' and enclose a copy of the minister's letter explaining the government's support. Relevant trade associations received official government communications informing them of the importance of the programme and of securing preference on the shop floor for approved orders. Of course, abuse of these special arrangements could have severe implications on industry in general. To mitigate the dangers and manage the process, suppliers would maintain a register of companies applying the super priority rules. Although voluntary legal sanctions could be enacted, companies manufacturing items on the super priority list were given preference to labour, their accommodation, materials, and the equipment required to meet the demands of the programme.

After a hard war everything was in short supply. Wartime rations were in place until 1954, there had been a loss of labour and wartime methods were unsuitable to the emerging times. Aircraft were taking far longer from initial designs to final production and were either obsolete before they entered service or were only suitable for a very limited time.

Supermarine Attacker F1s on the company's South Marston airfield. On the right is No. 4 shop, on the left is No. 5 shop. *(Highworth Historical Society)*

To spread the benefit of the programme and to speed up development and production, Duncan Sandys requested that the large manufacturers extend their orders to subcontractors as far down the supply line as feasible. There were legitimate concerns that many of the smaller companies did not possess the tools and facilities required for the modern aircraft industry. Such a shortfall did not only affect the smaller firms.

Much of the equipment needed was produced by the factories of the industrially advanced and wealthy companies in the United States, unaffected by the need to geographically spread production, as British firms had been to combat the dangers and disruptions of the Luftwaffe bombing raids. The government maintained that the delivery of US-made tools would keep pace with demand but of course this was not the reality. Under government guidance some vital machines were being operated 150 hours a week, and engineers were applying all their ingenuity to addressing gaps and developing alternative production techniques. Production of the Swift required more machining than earlier aircraft and Vickers Supermarine set up an American-type production line and network with major parts being fabricated at South Marston, near Swindon,

TOP TO BOTTOM
Main spars under construction at
Boulton Paul Limited. *(Boulton
Paul Association);*
Wing pairs on the production floor
on 15 February 1954. *(Boulton
Paul Assocation);*
A very busy view of Swift wings in
jigs at the factory in
Wolverhampton in February 1954.
(Boulton Paul Association)

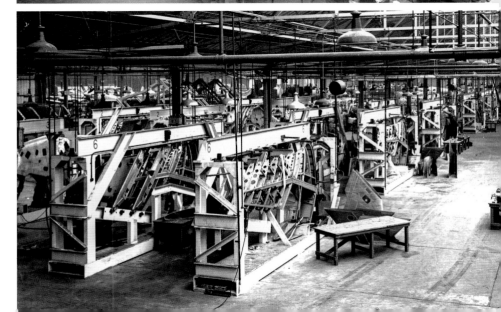

with sub-assemblies supplied by Boulton Paul, Shorts Brothers and Folland Aircraft.

Aviation Week of 27 October 1952 reported that the Supermarine factory at South Marston only had some of the machinery necessary to produce the Swift. There was a single Cincinnati hydrotel milling machine where six were required. Callers from the Ministry of Supply who visited the office of S. P. Woodley, South Marston's superintendent, were generally greeted with 'have you got my hydrotels yet?' These were table vertical milling machines used to accurately mill flat surfaces on metal bars, or castings or forgings in predetermined positions. One large spar miller was installed but there were no large skin mills on the production line. All the skin work was carried out on a small-scale converted machine, while Supermarine engineers worked at building a large-scale skin miller from 'odds and ends'.

Production of the English Electric Canberra was similarly affected. It was only being produced in a single plant until the vital Cincinnati hydrotels could be supplied to subcontractors Shorts Brothers, Handley Page and A. V. Roe. Across the industry there was a shortage of turret lathes, jig borers, vertical borers, and other vital machines, which led to talks around diverting some United States Air Force (USAF) stocks to the British.

Of equal importance was the need for an additional 75,000 workers required in the aircraft industry where technological advancements demanded far more skill than in the past. Although unskilled and semi-skilled labour was available, work could not begin without the recruitment of those with training in the new production methods. The essential numbers would not be achieved until 1955. Even at a simple level, Swift manufacture introduced new procedures such as wrapping some parts in tissue paper and racks were felt lined to protect the new high strength but sensitive surfaces.

A greater emphasis was placed on quality control and process management. Supermarine developed a method to check the standard of flat parts such as ribs. This tool used a surface plate with locating pins supplemented with sighting holes and raised areas. A fabricated part with matching locating holes would be placed on the surface and it would immediately be apparent if the correct tolerances had been achieved. Not only was precision manufacture important but every effort was made to reduce weight, where scalloped edges were used wherever possible on what would in the past have been straight edges.

The Society of British Aircraft Constructors (SBAC) is quoted in *Flight's* 4 April 1952 edition as stating:

> 'The society warmly welcomes the decision the government has now made to end the uncertainties which have so far impeded the achievements of the aircraft defence programme. Super priority [...] will run right down the production lines from the main contractors through equipment suppliers and subcontractors to the material producers [...] and will equally apply to those government agencies whose functions are an essential link in the specified jobs. The aircraft industry now joins in fullest co-operation with its official and industrial partners whose combined efforts are needed to make the scheme work [...] There are other types of aircraft vital for the defence programme itself which the government has not included in the super priority list, and there are exports of service and merchant aircraft which add greatly to our security and our solvency as a nation. The aircraft industry will use every means to draw in extra men, materials and subcontractors for this work, as they are freed from less essential activities [...] The government attaches the highest importance to exports of aircraft of all types, in which the British aircraft industry has an opportunity that must not be missed.'

CHAPTER 3

The Spitfire connection

IT WAS UNDERSTOOD EARLY in the war that an increase in aircraft performance was not merely a factor of engine power but was greatly affected by the flow of air over the wing. Supermarine had dived a Spitfire and reached Mach 0.9 but it was clear from tests like these that a new wing design would be required to take advantage of the more powerful engines being produced.

Specification No. 470 was issued by Supermarine in November 1942 with the aim to produce a laminar flow wing that would increase air speed and reduce drag. The principle of this wing was to delay air flow disturbance as far back along the wing aerofoil as possible and so reduce the associated drag to a minimum. With as thin a leading edge as possible the air only becomes disturbed towards the trailing edge; the result is that the surface area of disturbed air would be limited, as would be drag and any adverse effect on the control surfaces or flight characteristics of the aircraft.

A requirement for a new fighter was issued that would use a twin spar laminar flow wing; unusually the wing itself was given a type number of 371 and it was fitted to a modified Spitfire fuselage. An added advantage of the wing was that it allowed for the installation of a wider and more stable undercarriage. The first prototype, a standard Spitfire MK XIV fitted with the wing, was lost on Wednesday 13 September 1944, with pilot Frank Furlong. Although there was no definitive cause ever discovered, it was suggested that the aileron control rods, used instead of the cables typical of the Spitfire wing, had seized.

The second Spiteful prototype NN664 flew on 8 January 1945 with Jeffery Quill at the controls. It is seen here in June 1945 with the new five-bladed propeller, but still fitted with the original Spitfire tail. *(Crown Copyright, MoD. Courtesy of Air Historical Branch (RAF))*

The second prototype, NN664, was built to the Spiteful specification F1/43, which dictated a deeper fuselage, larger cockpit, and slotted ailerons. In trials, it exhibited some undesirable handling characteristics caused by the new wing and marginally higher speeds. More than a new wing design was needed to push beyond the transonic, and larger tail surfaces were fitted which improved the handling and lateral stability. A flying example and the possibility of increased performance encouraged the Air Ministry to place an order for 150 units. The Spiteful went into production as the Spiteful MK XIV following on from the Spitfire MK XIV from which it was first converted.

Mike Lithgow found the Spiteful, 'with its power-assisted ailerons and spring-tab elevator a great improvement on the Spitfire, the high-speed characteristics of the wing being especially encouraging'. Disappointingly there was only a marginal increase in top speed coupled with difficult low speed handling characteristics. It did however, become the fastest piston-engine aircraft in 1947 when Spiteful RB518 fitted with a two-stage Griffon 101 engine with a three-speed supercharger driving a five-blade propeller, was recorded at 494 mph.

With the extra speed, wider undercarriage and a seven-degree view over the nose compared to the Seafire's three-degree view, Supermarine proposed the navalised version of the Spiteful, labelled the Seafang to the Royal Navy. For naval operations, the vertical tail surfaces were redesigned, the fuselage marginally lengthened and provision was made to be able to deliver torpedo attacks. In May 1945, the navy issued an order for 150 Seafang fighters. Two full pre-production aircraft were built. These were known as Mk32s (VB893 and VB895) and were fitted with arrestor hooks, folding wingtips and contra-rotating propellers driven by Griffon 89 engines.

Neither the navy nor the air force orders were progressed beyond the eighteen Seafangs and nineteen Spitefuls. The possibility of the jet engine, with its increased power and speed, interested the services more than top end older technology. However, the last piston Supermarine fighter and its laminar flow wing would go on to make a significant contribution to the new Jet Age.

Before the first Spiteful had taken to the air Supermarine designers had laid down the outlines of what the chief designer termed his 'Spiteful development' to meet the 1944 Ministry of Supply (MoS) specification E.10/44, for a single-engine jet fighter. This first Supermarine jet-powered aircraft was designated as the Type 392 Attacker. It was to be fitted with the Type 371 laminar flow wing and the new Rolls-Royce Nene centrifugal jet engine, whose descendants went on to power a formidable foe.

Rolls-Royce developed and built their RB41 Nene engine within five-and-a-half months in 1944. The aim was to improve their current Derwent turbo jet engine to provide double the power. Instead of employing the reverse air flow method the Nene introduced nine straight through combustion chambers, fed by a double entry centrifugal-compressor, and driving a single-stage turbine. In September 1946, the newly elected Labour government in Britain approved the sale of Nene engines to the Soviet Union. The minister of Supply, Mr G. R. Strauss, confirmed to Parliament on 22 November 1948 that 'fifty-five jet engines were supplied to the USSR during 1947'.[2]

Despite reassurances not to copy the engines the Russians reverse-engineered the Nene and created the ubiquitous Klimov RD-45 that powered the Mikoyan-Gurevich MiG-15. Chinese MiGs captured in Korea were examined and the under-secretary of State for Air, Mr Nigel Birch acknowledged that these engines were

[2] HC Deb 22 November 1948 vol 458 cc839-41

[3] HC Deb 21 November 1951
vol 494 cc371-2

'copies of the Nene' and it was 'thus reasonable to suppose that the Russians have derived substantial benefits from the sale to them of the Nene engines'.[3]

The Nene technology was also sold to the United States engine manufacturer Pratt & Whitney, who licence-produced the Nene as the Pratt & Whitney J42, that powered the Grumman F9F Panther naval fighter, while in Canada, Orenda licence built the engine for the Canadair CT-133 Silver Star aircraft.

In addition to the Type 371 wing and Nene power unit the Type 392 comprised a new fuselage and a forward-positioned pressurised cockpit. A direct result of its Spitfire heritage was the decision to adopt a tailwheel rather than a tricycle undercarriage. Development of the new jet was delayed as the engineers worked to determine the elements of the laminar flow wing that contributed to the handling problems that had been experienced with the Spiteful. The sad loss of the prototype Spiteful further contributed to the delays in the wing development programme. Designers and engineers were working at the edge of current technological knowledge and it was only with the second Spiteful prototype that it was found that the higher speeds now achieved meant that the geared tabs on the ailerons became too heavy over 400 mph.

Famous test pilot Jeffrey Quill was at the controls of the Attacker prototype TS409 when it first took to the air on 27 July 1946. A direct result of the tail dragger configuration was that to avoid damage to runways and deck surfaces the jet exhaust pipe had to be angled slightly upward. The tendency to snake from left to right, identified on the initial flights, was addressed with the addition of a fillet ahead of the tailfin and airbrakes were added to compensate for the lack of propeller drag and provide a method to reduce landing speeds.

Mike Lithgow flew the Attacker prototype to Paris in March 1948 to demonstrate the new fighter to the French air force and navy. He was afforded the unique opportunity to fly down the Champs-Élysées at low altitude, passing over the Arc de Triomphe at 600 mph and returning to Hurn in under twenty-five minutes.

Technological developments first tried on the Seafang were incorporated into the second Attacker prototype TS413, to develop a navalised version of the new jet fighter. As with the Seafang it had folding wingtips, an arrestor hook, but in addition was fitted with strengthened landing gear and provision for a rocket-assisted

G-5-11 Supermarine Attacker carrying two 100-lb bombs and six rockets. The 1951 Farnborough report notes that this aircraft belonged to the Pakistani navy, although no markings are visible. The supplementary belly fuel tank was carried forward to the Swift FR5. (*Cliff Hall via Chris Hall*)

take-off. It was first flown on 17 June 1947 by Mike Lithgow. The tail surfaces differed to the first prototype, in that the tail plane was larger and the fin smaller, lift spoilers were fitted above the wing and balanced rather than spring tabs were employed on the ailerons.

Modifications were made continually to such areas as the wing, tabs, air intakes, fuel management, flaps, spoilers, all in an effort to manage flight in an unknown environment. The lack of funds, government pressure for jet-powered equipment and the need to manufacture a saleable product precluded the luxury of extended periods of experimentation and learning. The result was an innovative aircraft which did not quite meet its full potential.

In September 1948, 181 aircraft were ordered for the Royal Navy Fleet Air Arm (FAA). Armament was twin Hispano Mark V 20-mm cannon in each wing and additional range extending fuel could be held in the optional under-fuselage belly fuel tank. On 22 August 1951 the Attacker entered service with the 800 Squadron FAA at Ford, West Sussex, becoming the first jet fighter to serve with the Royal Navy, landing on HMS *Eagle* on 4 March 1952.

An improvement on the initial delivery was made with the Attacker FB2 which was fitted with a marginally improved Nene 102 engine and a framed canopy.

There was a single export order for thirty-six de-navalised Attackers for the Royal Pakistan Air Force. Fred Isaacs, who flew the Attackers in Pakistan recalls:

'Our check-out was conducted by Vickers test pilot "Pee Wee" Judge. It was simply being handed a copy of Attacker pilots notes to read, being asked if there were any questions and then into the cockpit to fly. There was no special protective gear available or issued at that time; you flew with what you had.'

Isaacs also noted that 'one had to be physically strong to perform aerobatics in the Attacker as without power assistance the stick had to be manhandled'. The new Pakistani jets were prepared for the 1952 Independence Day air display, performing a twenty-minute routine that ended with a spectacular vertical bomb burst split-up.

After short service in the front line with the FAA, Attackers went on to serve in trial and training units. Its low acceleration on take-off and reduced drag on landing made it an ideal aircraft for pilots to convert from piston to jet flight and to train deck officers, only being replaced when the mirror landing aid was introduced.

Mike Lithgow set a world speed record of 565 mph (909 kph) over a 100-kilometre closed course in the Attacker on 27 February 1948. However, it did not represent a major step forward in jet technology and, although in service by 1951 giving the FAA its first experience with jet carrier operations, it was replaced within four years by the Sea Hawk.

Attacker F1 WA485 was delivered to the Royal Navy in January 1951. It appeared in the film *The Sound Barrier* and on 5 February 1952, when attached to the A&AEE at Boscombe Down it crashed into a river near Leckford, south of Andover, Hampshire. The pilot Lt Cmdr Robert Malcolm Orr-Ewing attached to C Squadron (Armament Testing Squadron) was killed. *(Solent Sky Museum)*

CHAPTER 4

Swift prototypes

THE EXCELLENT BODY design of the Attacker and proven Nene jet engine was the obvious basis on which Vickers Supermarine could explore the boundaries of the 'speed of sound' and experiment with swept-wing designs. Realising the urgent national and company need to get ahead, Supermarine began work on plans to modify the base Attacker airframe. This in turn led the Air Ministry to issue Specification E.41/46 on 13 March 1947 for a high-speed single-seater fighter and a contract for two prototypes.

The prototypes, VV106 (a Type 510) and VV119 designated Type 535, were built at Hursely Park, which had been requisitioned by the Ministry of Aircraft Production (MAP) to accommodate the design and production departments of Supermarine after its offices at Woolston had been bombed. They were powered by the centrifugal Rolls-Royce Nene 2 engine, retained the Attacker's tail-wheel configuration and were the first British aircraft to have fully swept flying surfaces.

At this early stage, the first prototype had been given the name 'Swift' but unsanctioned by the Ministry of Supply it went into a series of test flights with the designation Supermarine 510. It was confirmed by *Flight* magazine that the company had announced that the 510 had been built to 'investigate the problems which are associated with flight at and beyond the speed of sound'.

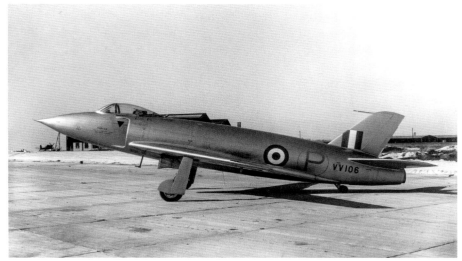

Type 510

On 29 December 1948, VV106 made its maiden flight in the hands of Supermarine's chief test pilot Mike Lithgow. Although unarmed, the design allowed for four wing-mounted 20-mm cannons.

In March 1950 *Flight* magazine commented that 'the 510 is the latest physical expression of a continuous line of aircraft which started with the original Spitfire'. The magazine traced the 510 line through the Spitfire, re-engined with the Griffon motor, modified with the laminar flow, thin sectioned, straight-edged wing, which came to be mounted on a modified fuselage, which was the ultimate Spitfire known as the Spiteful. All this ancestry could be found in the Attacker and had been further advanced and carried through to the

Type 510. The magazine presented a clear link to the Spitfire heritage in the positioning of the tail surfaces. The relationship between the tail plane mean chord and wing as used on the Spitfire had proved to be extremely successful and, understandably, the company wished to preserve this quality when designing the Attacker. Continuing with tradition the designers did not mount the tail plane on the fin, as had been seen on the Gloster Meteor and Grumman F9F Panther, but its low position relative to the main plane required it be mounted at a 10-degree dihedral or upward angle.

The tail planes, fin and wing had a 40-degree sweep, the maximum thought possible without affecting handling at low speeds. Unsure of their assumptions and obviously needing to provide control at lower speeds, the wings were fitted with fixed slots from the wingtip across three-quarters of the leading edge. As tests progressed these were decreased and finally removed, so confirming the low speed tip-stall calculations of the original design.

The fuselage width was determined by the Rolls-Royce Nene 2, a centrifugal jet engine, which because of the outer combustion chambers was very broad. Rolls-Royce calculated that a 6-inch gap between the engine and the fuselage body would provide enough airflow and cooling and be operationally sufficient. This then drove the location of the wing spars and thus the positioning of the tail surfaces, and aerodynamically determined the length to width and shape of the fuselage.

Fitted with a Martin-Baker ejector seat, the cockpit layout was neat and unremarkable, with forward of the bulkhead a substantial area for test equipment. The canopy and screen arrangement was, however, somewhat unconventional. Made of close to one-inch thick multi-ply optically flat glass, toughened to withstand bullets, the screen had in front of it an additional half-inch curved glass fairing. One of its roles was to maintain aerodynamic integrity, but as with the Perspex double-skinned side screens and canopy, this duplex glazing was intended to address the problem of misting resulting from differential between internal and external temperatures. The screen was directly vented, whereas the Perspex components were cleared through silica-gel desiccant packs.

Surprisingly, the tail wheel of the Attacker was retained, albeit with a twin set of wheels. At the time, it was thought that it saved weight and that the tail-down landing configuration provided enough drag to dissipate 50% of the landing speed aerodynamically,

In the air VV106 looked very much like the later Swifts. (*Solent Sky Museum*)

again saving weight and the expense of powerful braking systems. A direct consequence of the tail dragger configuration was that the flap training edges had to be reduced in size to allow for sufficient ground clearance.

Mike Lithgow wrote, 'it was obvious from the start that the high speed characteristics of this "new look" were exceptional, and in a matter of weeks we were flying at Mach numbers approaching .95, which was quite something in those days'. The 510 made its first public appearance in September 1949 at the tenth SBAC Flying Display and Exhibition held at Farnborough, where it was the fastest aircraft that year, recording a top speed of 670 mph.

A month later the aircraft was presented for testing at the A&AEE at Boscombe Down. The pilots found that the power-assisted ailerons facilitated a very good roll rate at high speeds but reported that a tricycle undercarriage and improved elevator control could result in a good fighter. Comparisons were made to Sabre F-86 and at high speeds the 510's performance was virtually equal to that of the American plane, only let down by its rather rough finish, no doubt a result of Supermarine rushing to catch up with the opposition. Handling concerns at low speed were raised when pilots experienced severe vibrations and a tendency for the nose to jerk five degrees either side of the intended flight path at reduced speed.

Vickers Supermarine 510 VV106 on the deck of HMS *Illustrious* between 8 and 9 November 1950. With Lieutenant Jock Elliot at the controls it was the first swept-wing aircraft to land on a carrier. Mike Lithgow and Lieutenant D. G. Parker subsequently also completed deck landings. *(Dutch Institute for Military History)*

VV106 was returned to Supermarine where the vibration issue was addressed with the removal of the 'needle' nose and replacing it with one from an Attacker and by increasing the air intake boundary layer suction through raising the exit louvres above the fuselage skin. Once returned to A&AEE the test pilots reported that it was easy and pleasant to fly and seemed free of any issues that could be expected from such a large sweep of the flying surfaces.

The Royal Navy's interest in a fighter with a greater performance than the Attacker, prompted Supermarine to fit the 510 with an Attacker-type arrestor hook and on 8 November 1950 VV106 made a series of landings and take-offs from HMS *Illustrious*. The first swept-wing aircraft to operate from a carrier.

Type 517

To overcome the shortcomings reported by A&AEE, VV106 was modified. The jet pipe on the 510 was angled four degrees upward and a moveable rear fuselage was fitted which provided a rudimentary variable incidence tail plane and was re-designated as a Type 517.

Further development flying was carried out until the aircraft was withdrawn from use in January 1955, having flown for a total of 230 hours and 40 minutes. It was assigned a maintenance serial 7175M and was used as a ground trainer at RAF Halton after which it was preserved at various museums. It is now held in the Reserve Collection of the Fleet Air Arm Museum at Yeovilton.

Type 528

VV119 flew for the first time on 27 March 1950 in the same configuration as VV106, but the rear fuselage was modified to allow for an afterburner and the air intakes were repositioned and made larger. The wing was redesigned to make provision for cannon and ammunition. Having modified the Attacker frame and proved that they could produce a flyable all-swept aircraft, Supermarine embarked on the next phase of development and grounded the Type 528 in May 1950 for an extensive upgrade.

The second prototype, VV119, at Chilbolton in April 1950. Mike Lithgow is in white overalls. *(Solent Sky Museum)*

Type 535

What emerged was the first real example of the ultimate Swift. The most obvious modification to VV119 was the lengthened nose which housed a forward-retracting nose wheel. Additional significant improvements were larger air intakes, a new canopy, and a reduced sweep in the trailing edges of the wing. The jet pipe was adapted to house a basic afterburner, which in turn necessitated a new tail cone to maintain the correct aerodynamic flows. Provision was made for guns to be installed in the wings but they were never fitted. Almost as a security blanket, it retained the tail wheels on which it could land to reduce the standard landing run-out distance and would automatically pitch forward onto the nose wheel at 75 mph (120 km/h).

The extensive research and rebuild of VV119 had been fully funded by Supermarine, while on the other side of the Atlantic, the United States treasury funded North American's multi-million-dollar Sabre F-86 development programme. Nevertheless the money had been well spent as VV119 became a valuable test aircraft.

After the first flight on 23 August 1950 it was clear that changes to the original design had introduced directional instability, which was rectified by the addition of a dorsal fillet from the tail across

Built as a modified Type 510 the second prototype, VV119, was modified to a Type 535 with a tricycle undercarriage; longer pointed nose; kinked wing leading edge; larger fuselage diameter (to accommodate an afterburning tail pipe); greater fuel capacity and provision for four cannons in the wings. First flown on 23 August 1950. *(Solent Sky Museum)*

VV119 taxies back to the hangar at Chilbolton followed by attendant engineers and ground crew. *(Solent Sky Museum)*

the top of the fuselage. Anti-gravitational pilot clothing was trialled, along with dummy Blue Sky missiles to study the effects of external ordnance on the flight characteristics. Aerodynamic tests were performed on upper-wing flaps and combinations of two or four gun installations.

Problems entering and innovating in the jet age that faced Supermarine were prophetically the storyline of the great box office success, *The Sound Barrier,* a 1952 film directed by David Lean. Almost a semi-documentary, it is a story following designers' and test pilots' efforts to fly at supersonic speeds and the problems they encountered. It was the twelfth most popular film in Britain in 1952 and received one Academy Award and three BAFTA awards in 1953.

Ralph Richardson starred as the owner of an aircraft company at the forefront of jet technology who had employed a famous wartime pilot, played by Nigel Patrick, as the company test pilot. The fact that the pilot was married to the owner's daughter added the necessary romance and conflict to the story. Of course, the film was a great vehicle to show off the British aircraft industry and there are scenes of the hero and his wife, played by Ann Todd, flying to Europe in a two-seater Vampire and of her returning on a de Havilland Comet.

David Lean placed considerable importance on fully researching the subject. He gathered reports on the effects on jet aircraft as they approached the 'speed of sound' and interviewed aviation engineers,

VV119 became famous as 'Prometheus' the aviation star of the film *The Sound Barrier*. Here it is being prepared for ground filming where the engine is run up and trees and bushes are battered by the 'power' of the jet. In the background is Attacker F1 WA485. *(Solent Sky Museum)*

designers and flew with test pilots. Pertinent and accurate was the depiction of the dangers and stresses that the test pilots faced daily. The fictional company's new jet fighter was plagued with problems and when trying to 'break the sound barrier' the Nigel Patrick character is killed. The film follows the family drama around this incident and the engagement of a new test pilot. This pilot at the crucial point of a flight carries out a counterintuitive action through which he maintains control of the aircraft and 'breaks the sound barrier'.

Named 'Prometheus' for the film, VV119 was the aviation star, with the supporting role taken by Supermarine Attacker F1 WA485. The aircraft were flown by Supermarine test pilots from Chilbolton Airfield in Hampshire. The story was very close to real life and pilot Dave Morgan felt that it was a good representation of the time, people, and the current state of the aviation industry.

In March 1952 VV119 was sent to Boscombe Down for tests to be undertaken on an air brake installation that was intended for the Swift F1. Test pilots classed it as an excellent system but advised that it did require modification to the control layout and operating characteristics to prevent its misuse at the wrong time. They found that with the air brakes extended the aircraft flew steadily and its use as a gun platform was unimpeded. Flying ceased for VV119 in 1955 and it was allocated instructional number 7285M, finally being scrapped at RAF Halton.

Type 541

In an interview with the Imperial War Museum in 1999, George Medal winner and Vickers test pilot Les Colquhoun highlighted the pressure brought to bear on Vickers Supermarine by the Air Ministry. Joe Smith, Supermarine's chief designer, had proposed that the swept Attacker would be a good interim fighter until the Hunter was in production, but the ministry was insistent that the older Nene unit be replaced with an axial flow engine. This set the whole programme back because such a fundamental change required the construction of a new prototype, the Type 541, powered by the Rolls-Royce RA3 axial jet engine that produced 6,500 lbs thrust.

This was an early version of the Avon series of engines which became one of Rolls-Royce's most successful designs, used commercially and militarily, with production finally ended in 1974. Work began on the AJ65 engine in September 1945 and the first prototype was started up on the engine test bed at Barnoldswick on 25 March 1947. A production version was delayed while engineers learned how to work in a new world of jet propulsion that combined high speeds with extreme temperatures, new metals, and unknown science. In 1950, the RA3, or Avon Mk101, fitted with an eight-stage compressor became the first production example. Similar engines powered an English Electric Canberra that made the first jet-powered non-stop Atlantic crossing and a BOAC de Havilland Comet that carried out the first crossing by a jet airliner.

Laid out on an engineer's bench is a technical drawing of an Avon engine with reheat from a Swift engineering manual. (*Tim Wood*)

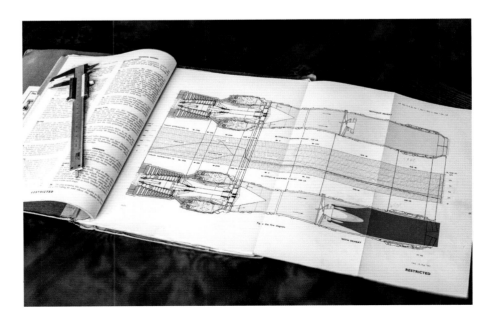

The Avon-powered pre-production Type 541 Swift F1 prototype WJ960. Built in 1951 it was retired to South Marston for ground-based trials and withdrawn in 1954. *(Solent Sky Museum)*

Two Avon-powered pre-production Supermarine prototypes were ordered on 9 November 1950, as part of the first order for 100 service aircraft. Designated Type 541 and allocated the serials WJ960 and WJ965, the two aircraft were not fully representative of the final Swift design but they were used to bed down the Avon engine installation and performance.

Both Vickers and Hawkers assumed a cautious tried and tested approach to solving the instability issues of swept-wing flight. Instead of adopting the idea of all-powered controls, a move taken by the American manufacturers, they stuck with what they knew using elevator spring tabs, along with aileron and rudder trim tabs to attain flying control. Government production demands forced their hands, but as Les Colquhoun observed it would have been far preferable to have spent the time, money and aircraft to construct the right solution from the outset.

Within two days of its first flight on 1 August 1951, WJ960's Avon engine shut down. On its third flight, vibrations in the airframe caused a break in the fuel system, a resultant automatic closure of a fuel stop cock and the consequential engine wind down due to fuel starvation. Mike Lithgow, who had been flying in formation with a Spitfire chase plane and Vickers Valetta camera plane carried out a very skilful unpowered landing at Chilbolton. Equally lucky was

Supermarine test pilot Dave Morgan who experienced another engine failure at 800 feet while on final approach to landing. Between him and the runway threshold was the River Test. Searching around for a suitable place to put the aircraft down, he in desperation turned away from the runway and into the wind, retracted the undercarriage, skimmed under some power lines and flew between a farm house and outhouse, which he struck with the port wing and then came to rest in the farmer's field. This put paid to the Type 541 at that year's SBAC show and it was three months before it was back in the air.

Booked to appear at the Brussels Exhibition, it was decided to use the occasion as an attempt on the London to Brussels records. WJ960 was fitted with smaller fuel tanks than the planned production models and Dave Morgan had to fly economically at a reduced height to ensure his arrival at the exhibition. His time on 10 July 1952 was a record 18 minutes and 3.3 seconds at a speed of 665.9 mph. A variable incident tail plane was fitted in August 1953 to experiment with aerodynamic forces, following which WJ960 was sent to South Marston to be used for engine trials. Only thirty per cent of the programme was completed before it was withdrawn in May 1954, because it was too dissimilar to the production units. It was then used for braking trials and finally runway barrier trials at RAE Bedford in 1956 before it was scrapped in 1959.

WJ965 was built to virtually production standard. It had a new canopy, less pointed nose, a modified fin, and redesigned air intakes. The main plane was positioned further back along the fuselage and incorporated Küchemann wingtips, designed to overcome the wingtip stall experienced at close to Mach 1 that increased the downward airflow over the tail plane and the inevitable pitch up of the nose.

Dietrich Küchemann served as signals officer in the German forces from 1942 to 1945 and during this time he continued his research into high speed flight, examining the effect of wave drag, swept-wings and initiated work on the fundamental area rule. Post-war he moved to the UK and worked at the Royal Aircraft Establishment (RAE) at Farnborough where he was pivotal in the development of a low-drag wingtip, which was a sweeping curve that ended at the trailing edge.

The idea of aileron spring tabs had been carried across from WJ960 and these combined with a weight-saving thinner-skinned

WJ965 was the second Type 541 prototype and built to virtually production standard. It had a new canopy, nose and the fin and air intakes were modified. *(1000aircraftphotos.com)*

wing, created a dangerous wing flutter. On one test flight the flutter was so severe and the twisting so great that the undercarriage dropped down and immediately pitched the nose up. This combined with the loss of the DH110 at Farnborough in 1952 forced the engineers to address the extreme dangers of wing flutter. The aileron spring tabs were replaced with geared tabs providing more positive control and after further test flights the braking parachute in the tail was removed which overcame the snaking movement that had been a problem from the start.

It was after this modification that Dave Morgan was able to thrill Supermarine staff when he achieved Mach 1 in a dive over Chilbolton on 28 February 1953, creating the first Swift sonic boom. It is reported that it was not long before the repeated sonic booms had become very unpopular with the residents of Chilbolton.

RAF test pilot Squadron Leader Noel (Ned) Lewis, DFC, took off from Boscombe Down at 0730 hours on 10 November 1953 to conduct specific tests in WJ965. These were to stall the aircraft in power on and off situations with and without the undercarriage and flaps extended, at between 15,000 and 20,000 ft. Ten minutes after take-off the aircraft was seen at about 3,000 ft and the engine was making 'a loud crackling noise'. Reportedly after another fifteen minutes the aircraft entered a flat spin from about 3,000 ft and crashed on Breamore Down, Hampshire killing the pilot.

Conditions were good, the aircraft well maintained and the pilot was in good health. However, in a stall condition the Swift was known to have a very high sink rate of 8,000 feet a minute and it was very difficult to recover a flat spin without applying power soon after entering the spin. There were no indications that the pilot had attempted to eject and it was assumed that he had remained with the aircraft beyond the point of possible recovery.

With only limited funds, Supermarine could not afford to build the number of prototypes that would have made the necessary significant impact on the development programme. There were no pure trial units available that could be tested to destruction. As a prototype was produced or repaired it was immediately employed on air trials. The first production aircraft embodied all the issues that had been identified while testing and no time was available to rectify these; instead service pilots flew under restricted speed and manoeuvring orders in place to avoid the known dangers of flight at height and at speed.

CHAPTER 5

Supermarine Swift

THE VICKERS SUPERMARINE Swift F1 had the distinction of being the Royal Air Force's first fighter with fully swept flying surfaces. It was the first fighter to carry the new 30-mm Aden cannon and the last Supermarine aircraft to serve in the RAF.

The Mauser MG 213C was a new gun designed for the Luftwaffe, meeting the requirement for a fast firing high-velocity 20-mm cannon. It was the British and French development of this gun over several years that resulted in the 30-mm Aden Mk4 cannon that equipped the Swift and Hunter. In fact, it was the standard British aerial cannon from the 1950s through to the 1980s, last in combat with the Sea Harrier and the RAF Jaguar. Initially produced by the Ministry of Supply's Royal Ordnance Factories and the B.S.A. Company, the name Aden was derived using the initials of the design organisation the Armament Development Establishment, Enfield.

Flight magazine noted the Ministry of Supply's announcement in March 1954.

> 'With this powerful cannon the Swift is capable of bringing to bear eight times more high explosive than was possible with earlier types of guns. Its revolutionary design gives the Aden cannon about twice the rate of fire of the 20-mm Hispano gun, which has been our standard fighter weapon since 1941. Trials have proved that the Aden, with advanced type of gun-sights and quick-acting fuse, is capable of inflicting devastating damage. The introduction of the Swift, with its

[4] *Flight* 25 June 1954

superb flying performance and terrific fire power, is a milestone in the progress of Britain's air defence.'[4]

At the end of the war the armed services were predominately equipped with piston-engine aircraft, but as another war seemed unlikely the decision was taken to delay re-equipping until 1957. In the meantime, the services could consider their requirements and produce plans for their development. As stated earlier, with the outbreak of war on the Korean peninsula there was an urgent need to upgrade RAF equipment. The demand far exceeded the ability to supply and the time frames were far too short to allow for proper and prudent development and testing. This was all too clear with the Swift where the decision was made to go into production with the Swift F1, before trials had been completed and faults rectified.

The government White Paper on the supply of military aircraft, published in February 1955 and summarised in *Flight* reported:

> 'In the fighter field a substantial production order for the swept-wing day-fighter was placed off the drawing board in October 1950, although its first prototype did not fly until nine months later. Several hundred more were ordered in the early months of 1951. This was later named the Hunter. It was also decided as an insurance to order off the drawing board an operational version, proposed by the makers, of a research aircraft, the S.535, which it was hoped could get into production before the Hunter; prototypes and 100 production aircraft were ordered in November 1950 and the production order was increased by fifty early in 1951. This was later named the Swift. Owing to the emergency, production orders for the Hunter and the Swift were placed much earlier in the development phase than would normally be the case.'

There was speculation in the aviation press in September 1952 that the large United States sponsored offshore purchase contract would potentially go to Supermarine. It was expected that 300 units would be ordered with production beginning in Britain but then continuing under licence to Fokker in Holland. However when the USAF chief test pilot, Major General Al Boyd, flew the Hunter and the Swift in November 1952, he reported that both aircraft needed improvement. He was disturbed by the wing stall evident in the

Swift and did not feel that it would be ready in time to meet the 1955 deadline. Accordingly, in January 1953 the Mutual Security Agency agreed to order 450 Hunters over the Swift as the fast fighter that would equip NATO air forces.

The Swift had superior flight endurance and Joe Smith planned to have modified the airframe in time for the Swift to be re-evaluated. To overcome Boyd's complaints, wing fences were fitted that eliminated the wing stall, the older Avon unit was replaced by the Avon RA-7A engine with afterburner and boosted power controls were installed. The F4 had an unbeatable climb performance and in June 1953 the first Hunter with afterburner had yet to fly. Both aircraft suffered engine surges and flame outs when firing the Aden cannon as the gases were ingested by the air intakes and the engine suffered oxygen starvation. When on 31 May 1954 the Swifts were grounded with an issue around the switching from mechanical to powered controls, the Hunter had been fitted with the same system and benefited from the subsequent resolution. Government reports stated that there had been 325 modifications made to the Hunter Mk1, which was considered a normal part of the development process. While the Swift still suffered handling problems the Hunter's air brake was completely unsatisfactory. It took three years and three designs before an effective airbrake was discovered.

Swift or Hunter?

For several months, the RAF had debated the merits of both fighters and in June 1953 it was reported that the Swift had been chosen over the Hunter primarily because of the greater range, but otherwise they were thought of as possessing very similar capabilities. Additionally, the F1 was due into service imminently, in fact ahead of the Hunter and would be modified to F4 standard over time. An order for 375 was expected to be placed, but that was not to be. In anticipation and to allow crews to become familiar with the new aircraft there was a limited release of F1s and F2s in January 1954. This was permitted on the understanding that there would be substantial improvements in later marks and that better control would be provided using the variable-incidence tail which was fitted to the F4.

The White Paper of 1955 went on to note that the Swift was based on a research aircraft intended primarily to explore aerodynamic problems:

'Subsequently, in the emergency of 1950, it was decided to turn it into an operational aircraft; in addition to introducing armament and all the rest of the operational equipment required for service use, it was decided to replace the Nene engine by the larger and more powerful Avon. The resulting changes from the original design so complicated the process of development as to become the basic cause of many of the difficulties which have been encountered. Production of the first mark with two Aden guns was ordered, as has been stated in November 1950; the first prototype did not fly until July 1952.

'The second mark, with four Aden guns, involving important changes to the wing, was ordered in April 1951 but a four-gun aircraft did not fly until May 1953; this was also the first aircraft representative of the mark 4 which was the mark for which the largest orders were placed for the RAF. The aerodynamic performance of all marks proved disappointing and great efforts have been made by all concerned to get the aircraft right. Meanwhile, as in the case of the Hunter, production has been rapidly building up. After a series of exhaustive tests, it has been decided that the Swift marks 1 to 3 cannot be brought to an acceptable operational standard. Within the past few days, certain modifications have been introduced into the mark 4. Further tests are taking place to see whether these have produced a sufficient improvement to warrant putting this mark into service with the RAF. It will be possible to replace the mark 4 Swifts by Hunters if necessary. Development is continuing for the time being of other marks designed for certain specialized functions.'[5]

[5] *Flight* 25 February 1955

Post-war technology had changed the shape of the aviation industry. Aircraft were far more complex. Bombers immediately prior to the war carried radio equipment weighing 150 lb in contrast to the V bombers which required 9,000 lbs of radio and electrical paraphernalia. Correspondingly the electrical power required increased from 10 Kw to 90 Kw. Development times were considerably longer, with the Canberra under development from 1944 to 1951 before it entered service, the Valiant from 1948 to 1955 and the B52, ordered in 1946 was not fully in service ten years later. Certainly, looking at the longevity of the B52 that gestation period was worth every year. The minister of Supply, Mr Selwyn Lloyd

[6] Hansard 2 March 1955 vol 537 cc2066-199

argued that the suggestion that there should be some central organisation to invigorate production was incorrect and that 'our difficulty was essentially one of development and not of production'.[6]

Supermarine conducted continuous tests and trials to overcome the handling problems but it was only in 1954 when a modified wing provided an improvement. The first three marks were inadequate as interceptors and additional Hunters were ordered to replace the shortfall created by the cancellation of Swift production. It was really at this point that the RAF or Ministry of Supply should have cancelled the whole programme, but instead the orders were reduced and Supermarine in consultation with the government reduced the industrial investment to save public funds in the event of a cancellation.

Only in February 1955 were those who gave advice on the viability of projects able to report that the possibility of the Swift matching the Hunter was very unlikely. There were no influential supporters of the Swift but there were still severe critics of the Hunter. In March 1955, the RAF presented three squadrons of Hunters in a display of strength, show of force and an indication of their faith in the new interceptor.

Production of the Swift was more expensive as the parts required more machining than those required for the Hunter and the unit price climbed ever higher. The purchase of the Swift was criticised by the Auditor General. The original order cost for 100 units was around £30,000 each but by the time the first example had been produced in 1952 the cost had increased to £43,000. By February 1955 only thirty-nine aircraft had been delivered, at which point it was realised that the first three marks were useless and that despite corrective action the F4 did not perform well at height. The original large order was reduced to only 170 airframes, and only 129 were delivered. By 1957 all hope for further development of the Swift was gone and the expenditure of £40 million was thought of as largely wasted. The minister of Supply, Mr Selwyn Lloyd, concluded: 'To sum up, the production of this aircraft was ordered off the drawing board, only two prototypes were ordered, there was no development batch, and a number of accidents retarded the development processes.'[7]

[7] Hansard 2 March 1955 vol 537 cc2066-199

Swift F1 WK194 was the production variant and first flew on 25 August 1952, powered by an Avon 108 engine armed with two Aden 30-mm cannon. It was delivered to the RAF on 31 October 1952, where it was assigned to A&AEE Boscombe Down until 1956. *(Solent Sky Museum)*

Type 541 Swift F1

The first two aircraft, WK194 and WK195, delivered against the government's November 1950 order for 100 Swifts, were built at Supermarine's Hursley Park experimental department. Mike Lithgow was at the controls of WK194 for its first flight on 25 August 1952.

Both aircraft were allocated to test programmes at Boscombe Down, Farnborough and with Supermarine. The first flight made by Squadron Leader Chris Clark, of the A&AEE, in November showed that the aircraft required considerable rework to be suitable for service use. With tests complete WK194 was scrapped in late 1956, while WK195 was modified as the F3 prototype.

Swift production was allocated to the South Marston factory where the first aircraft off the production line in March 1953 was WK196. Components arrived at South Marston from all over the country. The Supermarine factories at Eastleigh and Itchen provided smaller parts, Boulton Paul in Wolverhampton built the wings, while famous coach builders Thomas Harrington Limited supplied the nose of the aircraft. Production ended after only twenty examples had been built.

One morning in April 1953 the Duke of Edinburgh landed a Viscount 700 at Chilbolton. When he descended from the aircraft he and his party were greeted by chief designer Joe Smith and introduced to Vickers test pilots, and then were taken into the

RAF crews collect the first F1 fighter to enter RAF service from Supermarine's South Marston site. No.4 shop can clearly be seen in the background. *(Crown Copyright, MoD. Courtesy of the Air Historical Branch (RAF))*

flight test hangar. After examining the prototype Scimitars, he was guided to Swift WK194. He examined the two gun ports and gun camera in the nose and then sat in the cockpit and activated the flaps. He continued his tour talking to the mechanics working on VV119 and WK198.

In the office block, flight test equipment and results were explained before the duke and his companions climbed up to the roof of the control room to watch a display flown by Dave Morgan. He was scheduled to fly WK195 but it seemed that in a supersonic flight earlier that morning the jet pipe had been cracked and he had to transfer to his London–Brussels record mount WJ960. Morgan demonstrated the Swift with a high-speed dash across the airfield, at close to 700 mph and with a slow fly-past, but low cloud prevented anything more elaborate.

The visitors were driven to Hursley Park and were taken through the experimental hangar, lunched in the mess and driven back to the Viscount. Their journey then continued to the South Marston works. Here equipment used to extrude, stretch and shape the metals used to build the Swifts were shown and explained. Following that the group were taken on a comprehensive tour of the manufacturing line where they saw both Attackers and Swifts under construction. The duke was presented with a model of the Swift before departing for London.

Development work was hampered by a requirement to provide Swifts for the Coronation Review fly-past. Pilot hours were spent becoming familiar with the aircraft and valuable test time was lost. It was during these training flights in the June and July 1953 that the first of the recurrent engine failures was experienced. The Rolls-Royce Avon 105 engines, supplied only for the Swift, had been fitted with compressor blades made by a contracted supplier who made an unauthorised modification to the blade root fixing, which failed in flight, broke up and went through the engine. These failures, which took a while to understand, unjustifiably did a great deal to contribute to the poor reputation of the Swift.

Despite the engine problems, the Swift had pride of place at the RAF Review held at RAF Odiham on 15 July 1953, arranged to celebrate the coronation of the Queen which had taken place in June. There were 300 aircraft on static display and 600 in the fly-past. *Flight* magazine described the scene: 'At 460 mph came next six Swift F1s – a most welcome sight. Silently they approached, and noisily snarled past, dead straight as if along their own groove in the sky. They were noticeably more massive and rakish than the Sabres.'

Les Colquhoun remembers that at the time A&AEE pilots were clear that the inherent instability of the F1 meant that it was not acceptable as a service aircraft. Mike Lithgow recorded:

> 'The boosted flight controls had failed to overcome the inherent instability of the aircraft. At high speed in simulated combat, pulling back on the control column brought the nose up and the aircraft flicked onto its back. A wing fence was fitted to the top of the wing and the wing leading edge was extended forward, but the problem was the location of the centre of gravity rather than airflow over the wing.'

LEFT TO RIGHT
WK200 clearly showing the heavy-framed canopy and the large wing fence typical of Swift F1. This airframe was converted as the FR5 prototype in 1953. *(BAE SYSTEMS)*;

In the early 1950s it was the custom for a variety of RAF, RN and USAF aircraft to be flown into Biggin Hill so that members of the Royal Observer Crops and the Army Anti-Aircraft Command (then an integral part of the UK's air defences) could closely examine on the ground the friendly aircraft they were expected to recognise in the air. Here a Waterbeach-based 56 Squadron F1 WK207 'N' complete with the squadron red and white checkerboard markings attends the 1954 Recognition Day. It is accompanied by two USAF F-86s from Manston and a USAF B-45 from Sculthorpe. *(Tony Hawes)*

In October 1953, the Air Council decreed that 56 Squadron RAF would be equipped with the Swift and operational by the end of the year. Again, the focus was switched from development and solving problems to working up toward operations.

WK201 and WK202 were tested at A&AEE prior to the Supermarine's introduction of the F1 into service with 56 Squadron. There was a sense of urgency that the tests had to be completed at the earliest opportunity. Unfortunately, the F1 was found not suitable for full release. Despite this a release to service was granted by Controller Aircraft (CA) in January 1954, but it was almost with reluctance and certainly with severe restrictions. Most importantly the release was for non-operational use. Even in this role the flight envelope was restricted to below 25,000 feet, with a maximum speed of 550 knots up to 5,000 feet and Mach .09 to the upper height band. It was deemed unsuitable for any ground-attack role and pilots were banned from spinning their new fighter jet.

Exponent on and pilot of the Swift, Nigel Walpole wrote:

> 'Given its superior speed and with an element of surprise, it might have some success against first-generation fighters but not in a dog fight because of its large turning radius and loss of speed in the turn. [It was] concluded that the Swift F1 had four main shortcomings: poor operational ceiling, poor manoeuvrability and handling at high Mach numbers, a tendency for the engine to surge at low speed and high angles of attack, and poor rearward visibility.'

Type 541 Swift F2

There was a call to double the armament of the Swift, which gave rise to the F2, fitted with four Aden 30-mm cannons below the cockpit. Whereas in the F1 there was room for the ammunition bays, the addition of two more cannon required an alternative location from which to feed the weapons. Possibly because there was no alternative or maybe led by traditional thinking from the war, ammunition bays were designed into the wings. The modification required an extension to the forward wing root which dramatically changed the airflow. The F1's pitch-up characteristics were even more pronounced in the F2. Any turning manoeuvre at

A view of the South Marston
production line with WK243
under construction with other F2
Swifts. *(BAE SYSTEMS)*;
Swift F2 production line at
Boulton Paul Limited in
Wolverhampton on 25 October
1955. *(Boulton Paul Association)*;
A row of F2s freshly off the produc-
tion line. *(Solent Sky Museum)*

height with G force above Mach 0.85 would result in the aircraft instantly flipping on its back.

To overcome the problems Supermarine fitted wing fences to the outer upper surfaces but when these proved ineffective the engineers tried vortex generators. Wing or boundary layer fences are flat plates fixed to the upper surfaces of the wing, parallel to the airflow. They obstruct the airflow across the span of the wing and prevent the entire wing from stalling or losing lift. Vortex generators (VG) are small angled plates fixed to the upper surfaces of the wing and the angle of the plate causes the air to swirl, creating a vortex behind the plate. This forces the air to remain on the wing rather than separate from the surface and generate a stall. For instance, a

VG ahead of the ailerons prevents the airflow from detaching which would make the control surface ineffective.

Experiments were carried out on modified wing designs, including the later adopted dog-tooth leading edge. It was a while before it was realised that the real problem was that there was a shift in the centre of gravity because of the additional bulk of the guns and ammunition. To regain the correct centre of gravity, ballast was placed in the nose. This additional weight served no operational purpose and simply impacted on performance and range.

The test pilots at A&AEE were scathing in their reports, recommending a complete rethink on the design. Tested in 1954, WK214 and WK216 fitted with the Avon 105 engine, the extended leading edge from the wing root, armed with four cannons, were deemed to be below standard and worse than the F1. They were 1,000 lbs heavier than the F1, suffered from engine surge, and a lack of manoeuvrability above 40,000 feet. It was a condition of release to service squadrons that the A&AEE test pilots would need to visit the squadrons and advise pilots of the Swift's flight characteristics.

Les Colquhoun believed the F2 was marginally better, but agreed that the Air Ministry demand for four guns in the fuselage, the follow-on modified wing, and the ballast used to overcome the change in the centre of gravity resulted in limitations and handling problems that made it unsuitable for fully operational squadrons. The new reheat did not work properly, requiring the engineers to

spend hours adjusting the valves for it to even operate. This was indicative of the restrictions faced by British manufactures who often were over cautious themselves, continually underfunded and under extreme pressure from the government to produce jets to compete with the world and modernise the forces' air arms.

Les pointed out that Supermarine failed or were not permitted the time to fully examine the powered controls of the Sabre F86 and spend the necessary time and money to develop the right solution first time round. Hampered by a lack of money and development airframes, Supermarine had no alternative but merely to update production airframes with a variety of remedial actions in an attempt to solve ongoing problems.

WK219 and WK220 were used at A&AEE between January and April 1955 to determine the level of damage caused by the ejected armament links on the airframe. On both aircraft, several underside panels were replaced with stainless steel plates. WK220 completed six flights before it experienced engine failure at 27,000 feet on 16 March 1955 while being flown by John Crowley. Attempts to restart the engine were unsuccessful and it was written off following a heavy wheels-up landing. Tests on both aircraft proved that the new plates were unsatisfactory, suffering similar damage to aluminium plates and that the ejection procedure would require redesign.

BELOW
Swift F2 WK242 was delivered to the RAF in mid-September 1954 and served with 56 Squadron as 'P'. In 1955 it was sent to RAF Lyneham to 33 Maintenance Unit, and subsequently in March 1956 assigned as ground trainer '7302M' to RAF Halton. Two years later in May 1958 it was struck off charge but was substantially still extant in 1960 when this picture was taken. (*Peter Arnold Collection*)

Production began with WK214 and ended after only seventeen examples had been completed. Although some went to 56 Squadron many were never issued to the RAF. Six examples were sent to Australia to be used as targets for the Operation Buffalo series of nuclear tests on the Woomera/Maralinga Range.

Type 541 Swift F3

Another short production run followed that produced twenty-five F3s. This was the F2 modified with reheat and fitted with vortex generators on upper and lower surfaces of the tail plane.

None of the F3s entered service and only two went to Boscombe Down for trials. WK248 was used to evaluate the mark for Certificate of Airworthiness (COA) release over the period of November 1954 to January 1955. The pitch-up problem of earlier marks was less pronounced, no doubt a direct result of the effect of the vortex generators. Landing approach was far more stable, but engine surges were experienced in flight with or without the guns being fired. The only positive of the test report was that the F3 had a climb performance that was superior to the current British interceptors. WK253 followed as the next test airframe which was allocated to the Central Fighter Establishment at RAF West Raynham, before being re-assigned to the A&AEE where it was flown on tests until the October 1956.

LEFT TO RIGHT
Vortex generators on an F3 tail plane which was found by Chris Wilson of Jet Art Aviation. *(Jet Art Aviation);*
Swift F3 WK247 with reheat but without the flying tail in the Callum Muffler at Swindon. The nose wheel has been raised on a ramp to line up the afterburner with the silencer and powerful chocks positioned in front of the main wheels. *(BAE SYSTEMS)*

The other twenty-three Swifts were flown directly from the production line to RAF maintenance units such 15 Maintenance Unit, RAF Wroughton where they were assigned the M maintenance serial and allocated to various bases and technical schools, as instructional airframes.

By this time, the residents of Swindon and Highworth had grown tired of the noise of jet engines. They were regularly subjected to 140 to 150 decibel levels, significantly greater than the 120 decibels considered to be the threshold of pain. When the new aircraft were in post-production tests the noise from the reheat was highly disturbing to residents and workers alike. Damping the sound of a fighter run up to full power required considerably more ingenuity than that to silence an unfitted jet engine on the production floor.

Supermarine solved the problem with their first ground-running noise muffler supplied by Detuners Ltd of London. Known as a Callum Muffler S/A it was an open pen consisting of 12 ft 6 in high walls and sliding doors at the front, all lined with sound deadening materials. At the rear of the pen was the bell-mouth of a short muffler. The aircraft were reversed into the pen and the jet nozzle lined up with the muffler by using a ramp under the nose wheel and then its main wheels were chocked and the rear fuselage was attached to five-ton restraining wires. The doors would be slid closed and the engineers would work from their shelter built into the walls of the pen. This equipment reduced the decibels to 102 and it was quite possible to stand behind the muffler and watch the operation of the afterburner.

Type 546 Swift F4

The F4 incorporated not only the four Aden guns and the reheat of the F3 but also the saw or dog-tooth leading edge and variable incidence tail plane trialled earlier on the F2.

Jack Holmes, who began his apprenticeship at Boulton Paul in 1941 at the age of sixteen, recalls making the first prototype dog-tooth modification to the Swift wing in 1952. Included as an afterthought it was created by adding an extension to the outer section of the leading edge.

This highly secret work was carried out on a set of wings removed from the production line, by two shifts working night and day, with two men assigned to each wing per shift. Extension ribs

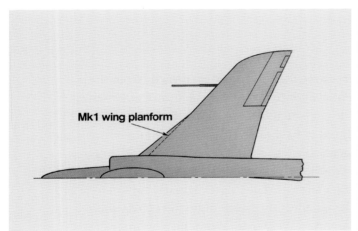

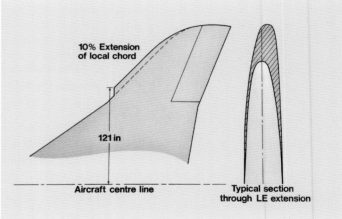

were machined from solid metal but they then had to be 'tailored' to
exactly match the skin contour of the wing. Placed at set positions
on the existing wing it was important that the wing covering was
not distorted as the integral fuel tank would leak. To achieve a
perfect fit the wing surface of each rib was painted with 'engineering
blue', left to dry, and then offered up to the skins; the high spots
would be indentified, which were then patiently skimmed down,
and with the aid of a feeler gauge the integrity of the wing contour
could be maintained. It would take perhaps a dozen or more fittings
before a perfect match was achieved, then the final assembly could
be completed. The final stage was a flow and pressure test. A sealant
was poured into the wing then placed in a frame which would be
rotated several times to ensure the sealant reached all corners of the
wing interior. Once the prototype wings had been approved they
were passed on to production and the new modified wing structure
was designed with the extension.

First submitted to A&AEE for testing in November 1954, WK242
was returned to Vickers as the longitudinal control was unaccept-
able when reheat was applied. This was rectified within two months
and the aircraft returned for testing and COA. The A&AEE F4
handling report dated 15 February 1955 was written up after test
flights with the first F4, WK272, which was fitted with an Avon 114
engine. This was the military designation of the RA7A Avon, with
reheat, as installed in the F3, which produced 7,500 lb of thrust.
There were many new features listed at the beginning of the report,
such as the availability of reheat, the variable incident tail plane,
and the one foot taller vertical fin to improve directional stability, if
a ventral fuel tank was fitted. The capacity of the rear fuel tank was
reduced to improve the centre of gravity, and it was noted that this

tank would be replaced by tanks in the wing leading edges which could hold an additional 50 gallons. The most significant change was the dog-tooth extended leading edge to the outer wing and the removal of vortex generators on the tail plane.

There was a marked improvement in the handling noted in the report. A tendency to pitch up, evident in earlier marks, had been overcome and the longitudinal instability improved to such an extent that any restrictions on the Mach number permitted was lifted. At the upper Mach levels, even the smallest level of input from the variable incident tail surfaces would result in a successful recovery of control, however if there was any movement on the elevator then the aircraft would immediately pitch up.

Approach control was found to be very satisfactory and significantly it was now possible to relight the jet engine above 25,000 feet. The F4 had a good rate of climb to 45,000 feet, in fact marginally better than any other British fighter tested. However, at the operating altitude of between 38,000 and 40,000 feet it lacked sufficient manoeuvrability and was considered as unsuitable for interceptor duties. Its controls did not provide the crispness expected of a fighter and it was recommended that the Swift would be outclassed above 15,000 feet. It was granted a COA but limited to 600 knots, and a weight of 19,500 lbs.

Record breaker

Unquestionably the most famous F4 was WK198. This was the third full production F1 to be built, but was soon after completion converted as the prototype F4, with full reheat, a variable incidence tail plane and wing fences on the main plane. It first reached prominence in the company of the F1s at the Coronation fly-past of 1953 when, following the single Hawker Hunter in the fly-past flown by Neville Duke, it was the blue painted WK198, piloted by Mike Lithgow that roared across the airfield with full reheat that closed the show. All the Swifts had been fitted with new engines for the fly-past, but Lithgow suffered total engine failure immediately after the review. He managed to convert altitude for speed and glided back to Chilbolton for a perfect landing.

On Sunday 5 July 1953, when piloted by Mike Lithgow the Swift took 19 minutes 5.6 seconds to travel from London to Paris, averaging

The week before the record attempt WK198 performed impressively at Farnborough in 1953. (*Air Cdre J. W. Frost via Peter Arnold*)

669.3 mph. After Dave Morgan's record flight a year earlier, the minister of Civil Aviation was questioned in Parliament as to why London Airport was used as the 'noise resulting therefrom was distressing to the residents of Cranford and Hounslow and that in many cases the noise, owing to its suddenness and unexpectedness, had the effect of causing nervous shock'. The rules of the Fédération Aéronautique International (FAI), the body that governed speed records, required that London Airport was the official point for city to city attempts.

> 'The aircraft had to pass low over the official observers at a height of less than 100 metres, to permit positive identification and to enable the timing apparatus to be started by the observers. After this the aircraft climbed rapidly; it crossed the eastern boundary of the airport at 1,500 ft. and continued to climb to 15,000 ft.'[8]

[8] Hansard 16 July 1952 vol 503

WK198 then participated in the air display at Le Bourget Airport before returning to London in 19 minutes 14.3 seconds, this time at a slightly slower speed of 664.3 mph. Although fitted with reheat it was not used on the record attempt which was flown at only about 1,000 feet. The previous record had been set by the forerunner to the Hawker Hunter, a Hawker P.1052 which in May 1949 recorded a speed of 617.87 mph.

Murray White, who had previously managed the jet aircraft carrier trials, was appointed manager for a world record attempt. He flew to

Libya accompanied by test pilot Les Colquhoun, supported by surveyors, and logistic staff, to select a suitable site.

It was important that the attempt was legally and technically watertight. Everything had to be prepared properly and measured accurately. White spent a day convincing the Ordnance Surveyor that a team from his office was vital to a successful outcome, despite the lack of authority outside of the UK. It was agreed that Supermarine would pay Ordnance Survey all travel costs, wages and provide a daily living allowance to the surveyors.

All personnel were based at RAF Idris, previously RAF Castel Benito. This airfield was constructed by the Italian air force and then, following capture was under RAF control from 1943 until 1966. It was used as a base for RAF squadrons on exercises over the bombing ranges in the desert. It is now known as Tripoli International Airport.

Les Colquhoun had previously selected a suitable location and after a survey it was agreed that the course would be a ten-mile stretch across the Al Aziziyah (Azizia) Plain. The actual speed reached would be measured between the 81st and 84th kilometre markers on the main road to Bur el Gnem, as it was then known. Preparations took two weeks. A full survey was conducted, mounting points for the measuring equipment constructed and phone lines laid down for communications at various points along the course.

On 22 September 1953, a heavily loaded Handley Page Hastings left the UK for Libya. On board were a full maintenance crew with an array of spares from a replacement engine to new windscreens and all the tools and supplies to enable them to keep the record attempt aircraft fully serviceable. Among the passengers were five men who would operate the timing machines and four official FAI observers who would verify the results.

As reported in the 2 October 1953 edition of *The Spectator:*

'One of the chief responsibilities of those international bodies which control speed records is to lay down a standard set of

Mike Lithgow arrives in WK198 at RAF Idris. *(Solent Sky Museum)*

conditions. For the world absolute speed record the Fédération Aéronautique Internationale's conditions are designed to produce speed figures which are truly representative of the aircraft's abilities in straight and level flight in still air and which are truly comparable between one aircraft and another. But the federation cannot standardise temperature, and this has become a critical factor. Temperature differences can take away or put on many miles an hour. Hence the desire of Squadron Leader Neville Duke, of Lieutenant Commander Lithgow and of the American challengers to make their speed runs in places where temperatures are high.

'It has been suggested that the speed figures obtained by the aircraft should subsequently be adjusted to a standard temperature; but this has the serious defect that the record would then become more a calculation than an actuality. At present the beauty of the official world record is that the aircraft's passage over the three-kilometre base is measured by observers outside the machine, using apparatus entirely independent of the aircraft's own instruments. It is a direct and independent observation.'

LEFT TO RIGHT
Along the course were sighting points and cameras. *(Fédération Aéronautique Internationale);*
The timing hut was situated at the eastern end of the course. *(Fédération Aéronautique Internationale)*

The paper's air correspondent went on to note that 'when aircraft reach the point of being able to blast their way through Mach 1 to supersonic speed, straight and level, the relative importance of ambient temperature will be much reduced'.

Surprisingly, in view of the importance of the record attempt, the week immediately before flying to Libya Mike Lithgow had

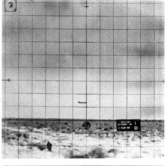

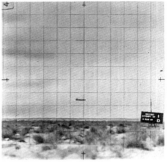

ABOVE, TOP AND BOTTOM
Four cameras, two at each end of the course, were connected to an electronic timing recorder. An operator would sight the aircraft through a telescope and trigger the camera as the aircraft crossed the start point. At the other end that operator would stop the camera as he sighted the aircraft cross the end marker. Lithgow pointed out that a faction of a second error in this process could create an error of 20 to 30 mph on a tracked speed of 740 mph. (*Fédération Aéronautique Internationale*)

RIGHT
Lithgow is cooled off in the cockpit in the shade of the hangar while waiting the 'all ready' signal from the range. The cooling system worked well on the ground but was ineffective in the air, where Lithgow had to endure cockpit temperatures of up to 180 °F. (*BAE SYSTEMS*)

been displaying WK198 in a series of vigorous routines, in preparation for and at the annual Farnborough Air Show.

Accompanied by Colquhoun in an Attacker Lithgow, in WK198, took off from Chilbolton for RAF Idris, making fuel stops at Nice and Tunis. Even before they landed the first of the problems that would bother the team, had arisen. The Hastings had diverted to Marseille with a faulty engine. A day was lost as repairs were undertaken and when it arrived the vital timing equipment was rushed out to the desert and installed on the especially constructed plinths set 1,000 yards off the road.

The FAI rules required that the aircraft carried out four flights across the measured three-kilometre course, two in each direction, the height of which must not exceed 100 metres. In addition, from take-off to the end of the fourth run, the maximum altitude could not exceed 500 metres. The speed was measured from the ground using cameras, telescopes, and timing equipment but the height measurements had to be monitored from the air. An Avro Anson and Gloster Meteor were fitted with sealed barographs, with the Anson stationed at the end of the course. The Meteor, with the necessary speed to monitor the Swift from take-off was then put on station at the start point.

Several groups of people began to gather at RAF Idris. Royal Aero Club observers, Supermarine's chief designer Joe Smith, Rolls-Royce representatives and a party of journalists who were kept at a distance to reduce the impact of a failed attempt and adverse publicity that may affect orders and production plans for the Swift. As could be expected the base fully supported the visitors, providing accommodation, food, iced water, transport, and medical services. The latter were under Wing Commander (later Group Captain) Tony Barwood, who went on to become a consultant in aviation medicine and specialised in the development of survival equipment and aircraft escape systems for military aircrew. His research as head of the applied physiology section of the RAF Institute of Aviation Medicine at Farnborough, resulted in modifications to ejection seats that reduced back injuries and pilot fatigue. He looked after those not used to the heat and dry conditions, providing salt tablets and advice.

During test flights, several problems arose. Ground-to-air radio communications were ineffective, which required Les Colquhoun to be airborne in the Attacker at 5,000 feet to act as a relay station. Colquhoun also had to fly to Malta in the Anson where he obtained some smoke generators, to mark the start and end of the course, which had proved difficult to see at low level at speed. Temperatures in the unconditioned cockpit reached 82 °C (180 °F) and Lithgow's refrigeration suit failed to cool him sufficiently. Often, he was so exhausted from the heat that he had to be lifted from the cockpit and it is astounding that he could fly a high-powered aircraft in such conditions.

On the first day of trials the fuel gauges failed and Lithgow was forced to reduce his run-in to the course with full reheat from eight miles to four miles, which meant he found he was still accelerating over the three-kilometre course. He also found that the inlet valve of the oxygen mask became jammed with perspiration and after a time on each flight he had to take it off to be able to breathe. Added to this complication was that the microphone was in the mask and he had to lift it up to communicate, an unneeded additional task in an already busy cockpit. Despite the smoke markers Lithgow found it difficult to see the start and end points. Luckily the Aero club members managed to make them more obvious for the following runs.

Ahead of the planned Saturday attempt the Supermarine and Rolls-Royce engineers worked through the night to fit new gauges

that had been flown out and modify the
rather elaborate cooling suit to make it
more efficient. For the record attempts the
wing fences had been removed, but there
had been no attempt to fill the screw
heads that had held them in place or small
gaps in wing and fuselage joins, vital
details that may have made a difference.

On the morning of 26 September 1953
WK198 was fully serviceable and prepared for the first attempt at the world
absolute speed record. The flight was
over within fifteen minutes and everyone except the time keepers
plunged into the pools to await the three to four hours of calculations to work out the best speed achieved. Later it was announced
that the official recorded speed was 737.3 mph.

Mike Lithgow wrote that the air was bumpy, with the effect that
the top speed could have been as much as 10 to 15 mph off the
expected pace. They hoped that the next day would prove better.
This was not to be as after the run it was found that the timing and
camera equipment was faulty and spares had to be sent from the UK.

The cover of the souvenir booklet produced by Vickers reflecting the FAI recorded speed of 1,184 km/h expressed in mph. Note this differs from the official and average RAC speed. *(BAE SYSTEMS)*

This delay became a key factor in the ultimate result of the Supermarine goal to hold the world record.

While the time keepers had to spend valuable time aligning their equipment, flying continued and it was during this time that the Swift reached 748 mph but the reheat failed and the aircraft became unserviceable. Timing of the attempt now became a major issue. Any record had to be submitted to the FAI within 48 hours and if another faster speed was to be submitted from the same aircraft it had to be at least one per cent faster, in this case beyond 743 mph. The problem was that the Americans were known to be trying for the record at the same time, and if the British held off registering their best time they could have lost the opportunity of holding the record at all. This had to be balanced with having the new timing equipment set up and the reheat problem resolved ahead of the American attempt and being sure the upper limit rule would be met.

The highest speed was submitted to the FAI and the Supermarine Swift F4 WK198 was awarded the Absolute World Speed Record. The Royal Aero Club issued the following statement:

> 'The RAC announces that Lieutenant Commander Lithgow attained an officially observed average speed of 737.3 miles an hour (1,183 kilometres an hour) over the official three-kilometre course, Azizia, in a Swift F4 Rolls-Royce Avon-engined aeroplane. Speeds attained over the course were 743.6, 729.5, 745.3, 730.7mph. The RAC has been asked to observe officially further runs.'

Further efforts to increase the registered speed were delayed when the desert Ghibli wind whipped up a two-day sandstorm. Within two hours of it dying down on the Friday, the Swift was in the air but once again the reheat failed and Lithgow returned to RAF Idris. At this point they heard that the US Navy Douglas XF4D-1 Skyray had already claimed a new record. Although their record had been lost, the team returned in the Hastings to Lynham satisfied that they had achieved their goal.

Despite attempts to limit poor press coverage, *Flight* magazine of 16 October commented that 'although the Supermarine expedition to Libya to capture the world's speed record may be deemed to have succeeded, there is no doubt that it did so only up to a point; for the speeds achieved by the Swift were well below those expected by Lt-Cdr. Mike Lithgow and the Supermarine team as a whole. In fact, the average of 737.3 mph submitted to the FAI, was originally considered as a try-out only, so confident were Supermarines that something well over 740 mph was not only possible but probable.' In the same article, they praised Mike Lithgow's cheerful demeanour: 'Despite extremely trying conditions, disappointments, and delays, he never once showed signs of temperament. He showed extreme consideration for the ground crews, who he realized were doing all they could to get the aircraft right. Lithgow always had a joke ready, although beneath his good humour he must have felt pretty mad.'

In May 1957 WK198 was retired, renumbered with maintenance code 7428M and assigned as ground trainer to RAF Weeton and then on to RAF Kirkham. Here it was used by No. 10 School of Technical Training, but when the base closed on 31 December 1957, WK198 was sold to Unimetals, a scrap dealer of Failsworth. It lay in the yard deteriorating and severely damaged until in 1981 members of the North East Aircraft Museum (NEAM) visited the scrapyard which was about to be cleared under a compulsory purchase order, and the aircraft about to be scrapped, along with two other Swifts. On 17 May 1981 a loan agreement was signed for the fuselage. When this agreement terminated the partially restored airframe was moved to the RAF Millom Museum in 2008. When that museum closed, the loan was transferred to the Brooklands Museum, where WK198 will be displayed in a restored Bellman Hangar as part of Brooklands Aircraft Factory exhibit on aviation production at Brooklands over eighty years.

Type 549 Swift FR5

The Ministry of Supply had completed the evaluation of the various marks of the Swift and it had been unofficially suggested that the Swifts might be used in modified form for ground attack or reconnaissance. The Gloster Meteor PR9s were obsolete and had suffered structurally from continual low-level work. Delivered in March 1950, they were first-generation jets with two Derwent engines delivering 3,500 lbs each and a top speed of 592 mph. The Swifts produced 9,500 lbs thrust with reheat and although only six years younger, were considerably advanced.

In this very posed shot, two airmen are holding a Vinten F95 70-mm film strip aperture camera. The F95 was developed for high-speed, low-altitude, oblique reconnaissance photography to be able to operate from second-generation fast jets operating at low level. The aperture provided an exposure time up to 1/2,000 second providing four to eight exposures per second. Both cameras are shown without their film magazines, which could hold 475 exposures and with the smallest lens weighed 16 lbs. Early versions were provided with either a 4-inch or 12-inch lens, while the later versions had smaller lenses and with the Mk10 1,200 exposures and all types had a 2.25-inch square image size. (*Ron Mortley*)

Swift F1 WK200 was upgraded to become the first Swift FR5. The nose was extended to house three F95 70-mm cameras, one in the extreme nose and two on either side ahead of the intakes behind oblique camera windows. These were either four- or eight-frame a second units that provided excellent overlapping images, which was a unique capability in the very low, very fast environment in which they operated.

To compensate for the longer nose, the fin was made taller to provide improved lateral stability. It carried the variable incidence tail plane, the dog-toothed main plane, pioneered by the F4 and a clear view canopy providing very good visibility. Although it carried 778 gallons, 500 gallons in the rear fuselage, 98 gallons behind the cockpit, and 90 gallons in each wing root, its flight duration could be extended with the addition of a 220-gallon belly tank, which could be jettisoned when a pilot found himself in a tight situation. The armament was reduced to a pair of 30-mm Aden cannons, while provision was made for external weapons mounted on under-wing hard points.

Roy Rimington remembers:

'Apart from the major difference of reheat on the Mk5 there were many other refinements which made it a more comfortable aircraft to fly. It had an all-round vision Perspex canopy compared with the part metal canopy of the F1 and F2 which gave only 270 vision. The control column grip was reduced in diameter to make it a more normal fighter grip similar to the Hunter, whereas the early marks have a very large cumbersome grip that was difficult to hold. The power control selection as improved from a purely electrical switch selection on the F1, modified later to a crude manual selector, to a positive push rod system which combined with a red and green light display, gave a positive indication of power engagement. Entry to the cockpit was made easier with a removable ladder as opposed to spring-loaded toe grips in the earlier versions.

'The ailerons on the FR5 however were much improved. The F1 and F2 aileron power system was the same as the Hunter. However, the FR5 had an improved booster system which gave much better balance and cut out the knife-edge control feel of the earlier system. There were other differences in the cockpit purely connected to the aircraft role such as camera switches for the two oblique F95 cameras and the nose camera. There was also an extra dolls eye for the ventral tank which went white when empty or no longer transferring fuel.

'It is difficult to compare the flying characteristics clearly because we had restrictions on the F1 and 2 and we did not fly regularly. In the year it was in service only twelve per cent of my total flying was in the Swift. Everyone was overly cautious of the fact that it was the first swept-wing fighter on the Royal Air Force and even our logbook times were recorded by air traffic control to the nearest minute from take-off to touch-down. As well as the improvement in aileron control the turning performance of the FR5 was superior. The F1 had a tendency to dig-in at high G but this was completely eliminated in the FR5 due to the dog-tooth leading edge. The F1 only had a boundary layer fence while the F2 had additional vortex generators outboard of the fence. Another advantage of the FR5 was the variable incidence tail plane compared to the conventional tail plane of the F1 and F2. The airbrake/flap design did not change, I am pleased to say, and was the most effective of all aircraft I had flown. This experience, however, was limited to the Swift/Hunter era. There was a limit switch on the instrument panel for selecting full flap (50) or take-off/airbrake (35 max). However, there was an inching switch on the throttle unlike the in/out control of most airbrakes. This gave excellent control of turn and speed by using small blips of airbrake/flap.

'We never attempted to fly the FR5 in the interceptor role but as a gun platform low level in both air-to-air and air-to-ground it was excellent. There is no comparison with the earlier marks because we were restricted in the use of cannons. However, the Swift really excelled in the low-level reconnaissance role. Fully fuelled with ventral tank it had to be treated with respect, especially when taking off from a short runway on a hot day, but at higher speeds it was

A line-up of FR5s of II (AC) Squadron at Geilenkirchen, Germany with ground crews ready to assist pilots to prepare for flight. No squadron markings had yet been applied. *(Solent Sky Museum)*

comfortable and stable even at very low level which made it ideal for the fighter-recce role. The difficulties of map reading at high speed low level were considerably reduced by the stability of the aircraft even in the most turbulent conditions. Without the ventral tank it was a joy to fly and an aircraft in which one could feel totally comfortable.'

Roy's report is supported by Nigel Walpole, who in an interview with the Imperial War Museum commented that the Swift was very stable due to its 'wonderful ailerons and you could fly almost hands off at low level and in that sense, it was better than the Hunter'.

The FR5s were the pioneers of the low-level, high-speed reconnaissance flights under enemy radar and played an important part in the development of terrain-following radar that today is essential for low-level aerial missions. On two occasions the aircraft won the annual NATO reconnaissance competitions. It was a solid, fast ride down in the treetops and, despite the unreliability of the fighter Swifts, turned out to be very strong and trustworthy.

Tested at Boscombe Down in July 1953, the first production versions flew in 1955 and then in January the following year the first operational units were issued to II (AC) Squadron based at Geilenkirchen in Germany. Within a year, *Flight* magazine reported on the success of the Swift in its new role. The 14 December 1956 issue described how the commander-in-chief of the 2nd Tactical Air Force believed the reliance on nuclear weapons to win a war was dependant on 'adequate and speedy reconnaissance to locate suitable targets' and that the Swift was of 'supreme importance'.

Having become somewhat of an expert in the Swift, Roy Rimington performed with the FR5 at several air shows. He wrote:

'I would select reheat for the take-off run and bring the throttle back out of the gate to the full position. Reheat was therefore still on to give maximum acceleration. At about 110 kts I would cancel reheat with the reheat switch but still at full throttle. Then at about 120–125 kts, I would put the throttle through the gate to reselect reheat and immediately raise the undercarriage. This almost always occurred opposite the crowd enclosure and gave a bang with an almost rocket-like take-off. (Very tame compared to present-day aircraft.) I would then turn away from the crowd through 270 degrees with reheat burning and, hardly climbing, the aircraft would reach and hold about 300 kts in a max rate turn at about 5 G. Just before the 270-degree turn was complete, I would cancel reheat again with the switch and perform a Derry turn, reselecting reheat as the aircraft was opposite the crowd flying along the runway reciprocal.

'Whenever reheat was selected I would always bring the throttle back through the gate so that the switch was operative for cancelling and the throttle in the right position for reselection. I followed this by a Derry turn in the opposite direction and then two half loops and a full loop, making a clover-leaf pattern, cancelling reheat and reselecting it opposite the crowd on each manoeuvre. This was followed by a straight and level inverted run and slow roll and here the Swift's excellent aileron control was a tremendous advantage. One could take up the whole length of a 2,000-yard runway at 270 kts in a slow roll with hardly any variation in height. For the finale I would fly out about 5 miles accelerating all the time in reheat and fly downwind along the runway by which time I could reach about Mach 0.9. Just before pulling up to the vertical opposite the crowd I would cancel reheat and then reselect on the pull up.

TOP TO BOTTOM
FR5 XD916 of II (AC) Squadron based at Geilenkirchen pictured on 15 June 1956. *(Crown Copyright, MoD. Courtesy of Air Historical Branch (RAF))*;
A grainy shot of a 79 Squadron FR5 in its element very low over Germany. *(Sandy Burns)*

I could then manage about seven complete vertical rolls before reaching the minimum speed at about 19,000 ft, quite often out of sight and above cloud. One particular aircraft which I always tried to use had a habit of dumping fuel in the high G pull up which would ignite when reheat was selected. This, I am told, gave a most spectacular firework display but was a source of concern to our engineering officer who could find nothing wrong with the aircraft.'

Les Colquhoun in his interview with the Imperial War Museum felt that the Swift came into its own in the reconnaissance role. He commented that it handled very well at very low altitudes and at high speed. It was stable and immensely strong and the pilots thought it was a lovely aircraft.

Only ever operated in Germany against the perceived greatest threat to the western world, there were never sufficient aircraft to maintain serviceability and by November 1957 the Swifts were being replaced by the Hunter FR10.

Type 552 Swift F7

Towards the end of the war the Ministry of Supply, the Air Ministry, War Office, and Admiralty combined to map out the future strategy for weapon development and rearmament. Britain's economy was in a weakened state and unlike the United States the defence officials had to carefully select which type and quantity of weapons they could afford to explore. A ten-year plan was laid covering the period from 1947 to 1957, at the end of which the V bombers would have been delivered, along with the first British guided missile.

Originally known as Blue Sky, the Fireflash missile was, compared to today's aircraft weapons, a relatively simple system, as 'homing' mechanisms had yet to be developed. Manufactured by

Fairey Aviation it consisted of three main parts; the missile and two solid fuel rocket boosters mounted on the forward fuselage. As the missile was not powered to the target it had a limited range but at the time it was thought that the rocket exhaust would interfere with the radar beam. Within 1.5 seconds of launch the boosters were explosively jettisoned leaving the unpowered missile travelling at Mach 2. It was then guided to the target 'riding' a narrow radar beam emitted by the launch aircraft towards the target.

The aircraft gunsight was synchronised to the radar beam and to keep the missile on target the pilot would have to keep the target in the sight throughout the attack. Located in the rear of the missile, the guidance system would search for the centre line and then use pneumatic servos, operated by solenoid valves, to control the missile's four rudders and keep it on track. A compressed-air bottle provided power to the servos and the inertial navigation system, while air from the aircraft was used to spin the gyros before launch. The warhead was housed in the extreme nose of the missile and this used an early proximity fuse as a trigger.

Ground-based trials of the weapon were successful and No. 6 Joint Services Trials Unit was established in 1955 at RAF Valley to continue these tests and to develop the protocols around working with guided weapons. On 16 May 1956 Lord Carrington, the minister of Defence, announced in Parliament that it 'was never intended or

TOP TO BOTTOM
Fitters push two Fireflash
air-to-air missiles on trollies to be
loaded under the wings of F7
XF120 of the guided weapons
development squadron at RAF
Valley on 8 October 1958.
(Crown Copyright, MoD. Courtesy
of Air Historical Branch (RAF));
XF119 armed with two Fireflash
missiles on a trial flight from RAF
Valley. (BAE SYSTEMS)

9 Hansard 16 May 1956 vol 197
cc474-99

contemplated that all marks of the Swift would be cancelled, and a small number of these aircraft will be used for trials of the air-to-air guided weapon, Fireflash'.[9] In February the following year, the minister of Supply Mr Reginald Maudling announced that it was always intended that the Swift would be the first aircraft to carry guided missiles.

Knowledge of guided missiles was rudimentary in the early 1950s and the design work to fit the missiles, their release mechanism and the radar equipment to an aircraft required a great deal of ingenuity. An order was placed for twelve Swift F7 aircraft to be used exclusively in the development of missile technology, to work out the tactical application of missiles and the creation of techniques needed to manage missiles within an operational squadron. Development was to be carried out by the guided weapons development squadron (GWDS) at RAF Valley run jointly by Fighter Command and the Air Ministry through Central Fighter Establishment.

Two or four Fireflash missiles could be mounted under the wings of the F7. Overall the F7 was marginally larger than the earlier Swifts, with the fuselage 1 ft 6 in longer and the wing span stretched by 2 ft 8 ins. All other armament had been removed and replaced with fuel tanks, extending its range by 235 miles. In the nose, a fixed-dish radar was installed with behind that an early computer to manage the firing sequence and other aircraft-to-missile services.

Along with thirty-seven other RAF stations RAF Valley invited the public in for an open day on 14 September 1957 and revealed for the first time the Swift F7. XF119, one of the aircraft of the recently formed No. 1 GWDS, was in the static display park, armed with two Fireflash missiles, while other Swifts of the squadron performed in the air displays.

Even before the Swift Fireflash trials began it was clear that the missile would not go into service. When Fairey requested an order for 1,000 missiles, its effectiveness was called into question. *Flight* magazine was reporting in 1957 that it was clear that Fireflash was an interim weapon and Fairey must have been aware of its limitations. Although the radar had a range of ten miles, firing would expect to take place at five miles but more typically only two miles from the target. All the tests proved that it was reliable and of course it had the advantage that it was largely immune to counter measures from the target. As the receiver was in the rear of the fuselage it would only take commands from the launch aircraft.

Swift F4 WK279 was converted as the prototype F7 and undertook the first successful missile firings in October 1955. It was tested at A&AEE and then withdrawn from service in July 1957 and a year

Three F7s airborne from RAF Valley. XF124 (centre) is armed with at least one Fireflash missile while the empty hard points can clearly be seen on the aircraft behind. *(Crown Copyright, MoD. Courtesy of Air Historical Branch (RAF))*

or so later scrapped. XF774 was the first pre-production prototype which first flew on 29 March 1956, with the second one XF780 flown in June. Both aircraft were sent to Boscombe Down for a programme of test firings. XF774 was only fitted with a prototype tracking and firing mechanism, while XF780 was the first aircraft to have the complete weapons system installed. The tests at A&AEE found that the weakest point was the aiming of the radar beam, effectively the command guidance of the round fired. The pilot had to keep contact with the target, which was feasible when attacking a large and slow moving aircraft but almost impossible on a fast fighter taking evasive action. Probably the most dangerous aspect of a launch manoeuvre was that the attacking pilot was committed to maintaining contact with the 'enemy' until successful contact and could not himself take any evasive action.

The first production F7, XF113 joined the other three, for handling trials, where it was established that the maximum permitted speed was 600 knots reduced to 580 knots when armed with missiles.

Under development at the same time as the Fireflash was de Havilland's Firestreak missile. This was a fire-and-forget weapon, a first-generation passive infrared homing missile. Initially known as the Blue Jay, the first firing took place in 1955 and it entered service as the Firestreak. Its adoption by the armed forces had been made easier by the intensive eighteen-month Swift Fireflash programme in Anglesey.

Launches over the Aberporth range were not designed to test the weapon, in fact on most occasions, to save money, the missile was fired when the drone was out of range and accuracy was rather calculated than observed. However, thousands of pounds and hundreds of hours were saved through the work at GWDS. There were twenty-four points of data gathered by the missile to record its assembly, handling, storage and firing and this information was analysed and methods of operation created to prevent errors, damage and misfirings in future similar systems.

XF774 was used for missile test firing trials by A&AEE and then struck off charge in August 1958, sent to 23 Maintenance Unit at RAF Aldergrove and then scrapped. Supermarine, Company Profile 1913-1963, states that XF780 was transferred to the MoS and was briefly designated as a PR7 suggesting cameras may have been carried in the nose rather than the radar at some stage, but by the end of 1957 it was withdrawn and then scrapped the following year.

The splendid Air Defence Collection at RAF Boscombe Down, records:

> 'XF113 returned to the makers in early 1957 for some modification work before being issued to the Empire Test Pilots School at Farnborough marked as "19" from July 1958 to July 1961. Retired in October 1961, she was used as a spares source for XF114 and eventually sold to a scrap dealer in 1965. The nose section was sold on, and Dr Robert Poulter acquired the nose, in poor condition, in the 1980s. Tony Dyer bought it and initially placed it on loan to the Boscombe museum, beginning some restoration work. Since then, however, the museum itself has taken on ownership of the nose and finished a full restoration which is on display.'

Ten F7s, XF115 to XF124, were used between April 1957 and December 1958 and were very successful in the trials. It was reported that some consideration was given to developing the Supermarine product as a high-level bomber destroyer but due for delivery were more advanced aircraft better suited to the task, such as the English Electric Lightning and the Gloster Javelin, and there was no further development of the Swift. The F7s were sent to 23 Maintenance Unit at RAF Aldergrove in 1958 and then in February 1960 sold as scrap to H. H. Bushell of Birmingham.

There is a single complete F7 survivor, XF114. Constructed in 1956 at South Marston, with the constructor's number VA9597, it was flown for the first time on 4 September. Delivered to C Squadron A&AEE on 14 March 1957, from 4 September of that year it was predominately used to test aircraft operations on wet runways.

At one time owned by Jonathan Whaley of Aviation Heritage, he recorded that:

> 'The first contract was 6/Acft/15373/CB9(c). There were preliminary instrumentation-proving trials at Wisley Airfield, followed by runway trials. Firstly, on a brushed concrete runway at Royal Radar Establishment (RRE) Pershore in 1960 and the following year on the same surface at RAF Station Coltishall. Later in 1961 a grooved asphalt runway at RAF Station West Raynham was tested to measure the effects of a rougher surface on braking efficiency. Further

trials on asphalt surfaces were completed at Upper Heyford and on an old asphalt runway at A&AEE Boscombe Down. The contract ended with trials on a concrete runway at Filton. A new contract, KC/W/063/CB9(c), was awarded on 16 February 1962, for "Aquaplaning and Slush Drag" investigations. These took place at Wisley, London Heathrow, Bedford, Weybridge and finally Cranfield.'

The report on the Cranfield tests opens with:

'The object of the investigations at Cranfield is to investigate the effect of water depth, surface roughness, drainage characteristics and tyre pressure on aquaplaning and tyre ground friction.

'Tests at Cranfield are full scale on the single main-wheel undercarriage of a Vickers Supermarine Swift F7 operated through ponds of water on a test surface. The test area is a precision surface, level to an accuracy of 1/16" over its entire width. The levelled area is built into runway 22-04 and consists of six different surfaces of varying texture, three of concrete and three of asphalt. The ponds are constructed of 1" T-section rubber strip affixed to the surfaces by suitable adhesives which were selected after a series of tests.

'The Swift is fitted with an A.22 recorder giving traces of port and starboard wheel speeds, obtained by means of wheel speed generators, and airspeed. A modification is in hand to record oleo leg extension as a measure of wheel load and hydrodynamic force.'

It is interesting to note that there was no performance data available for the Swift so the runs were limited to 140 knots, which allowed the perfection of the tests. Once the performance figures were supplied it was possible to replace the free run tests with fully braked tests which allowed a better understanding of sink rates and critical depths.

Under the dramatic headline 'A Fighter lands at Heathrow', *Flight* magazine reported in May 1962 on the 'landing trials at London Airport under contract to the Ministry of Aviation. Flown by "Dizzy" Addicott of Vickers-Armstrongs Aircraft, the trials were to gather data on braking in wet conditions.'

After a short spell at A&AEE, XF114 spent its remaining career on landing trials on various surfaces, wet and dry. Seen here at Cranfield in June 1966 where the main undercarriage doors have been removed to allow the engineers to fully record the outcome of their tests.
(*Jerry Hughes*)

The magazine remarked that the Swift had been selected because of its robustness and the strength of it undercarriage. Before the trials began it took engineers four hours to fit and calibrate the gauges fitted to the undercarriage to measure 'the side, drag and end loads, coefficient of friction being the drag force divided by the end load'.

To prevent skewed data the Swift was towed to the head of No. 1 runway while five bowsers sprayed 3,000 feet of the runway with 6,000 gallons of water. 'The Swift took off, completed a tight circuit at about 1,000 ft, and three minutes later landed at 200 mph intentionally slightly short of the wet portion. The small fighter, followed by a plume of spray, moved down the runway with little apparent loss of speed; then the spray died down as the dry section of the runway was reached and the Swift came to a stop.'

Ten tests were made over ten days. As this was a fully serviceable runway the tests had to be made to fit in with the commercial airline schedule. It was important that a live runway was used as all the tyre and oil deposits from the airliners added to the validity of the test results.

Results of the trials were to be compared to others which were to be carried out at South Marston, to determine if asphalt or concrete runways were safer, if grooves would raise the braking effectiveness in wet conditions and at what depth of water, speed and force of braking, hydroplaning occurred.

By the time the Heathrow trials took place, 'high hysteriesis' rubber tyres, similar to those used on racing cars, had been tested and it was already known that an increase in the number of wheels on an undercarriage did not improve relative braking and that coaxial wheels achieved better braking than an in-line configuration.

Jonathan Whaley reports that 'on 14 April 1967, XF114 was struck off charge and after brief storage at Aston Down, sold to Flintshire Technical College, Kelsterton as an instructional airframe. In the ten years of service, the records show that although she hurtled down the runway many times, she had only amassed 12 hours 10 minutes flight time!'

Replaced by a Jet Provost. XF114 was sold in the late 1980s to a private owner with the intention of restoring it to flying condition. Purchased by Jonathan Whaley in 1998, it was stored at RAF Scampton in a stripped down and a partially restored state. When it was subsequently put up for sale the Solent Sky Museum, previously Southampton Hall of Aviation purchased the aircraft. It is now in storage waiting the funds for restoration and the construction of a building in which to be displayed.

CHAPTER 6

Squadron operations

56 Squadron

Although not fully combat ready, the Swift entered service with 56 Squadron at RAF Waterbeach, Cambridge, with the arrival of WK209 on 22 February 1954 and introduced the RAF to the Supersonic Age. For the pilots, the cockpit was sophisticated compared to the Meteor and it featured power controls, airbrakes and, for the first time, pressure breathing masks and anti-G suits. The squadron's operations book records that 'Lieutenant Commander Morgan spent a week on the station and helped considerably with his advice'. By the end of the month three aircraft had been delivered. The first Waterbeach pilot to fly the Swift was Wing Commander Giddings, followed by Squadron Leader Storey. Deliveries were very slow with only five aircraft on strength by the end of March. This held up the conversion of pilots as those converted need to keep up their flying hours.

The first Swift emergency was experienced on 13 April when the first of many hydraulic failures occurred and Captain Bode was forced to lower the undercarriage, but it took time for the main wheels to lock and on top of that the aileron hydroboosters failed. During the rest of that month the squadron was engaged in firing

The first Swift delivered to an operational squadron was WK209, seen here on arrival at Waterbeach. *(56 (R) Squadron)*

These men were the pioneers of the operational Swift community. They are from left to right: Squadron Leader Storey, Flight Lieutenant McCraig, Flying Officer Martin and Flying Officer Harvie, with F1s and F2s in the background. *(56 (R) Squadron)*

and interception exercises, where on one scramble they intercepted a force of fifty Canberras flying in pairs.

Three aircraft were lost. The first ejection from a Swift was by Squadron Leader G. J. Storey on 7 May 1954. Flying WK209, he was forced to leave the aircraft at 10,000 feet when he entered a spin during stalling practice. The aircraft came down south of West Raynham, Norfolk. Six days later Flying Officer Neil Thornton was tragically killed in WK208 at RAF Waterbeach on his second Swift flight. It is reported that he lost control shortly after take-off at 600 ft. This may have been because of a 'false lock' on the controls which left him with very heavy unmanageable ailerons. When Flying Officer John Hobbs could not lower the nose wheel on WK213, he elected to eject at 8,000 feet. The aircraft came down on Hemstead Wood, Suffolk on 25 August 1954.

On 2 October 1954 Flight Lieutenant Hoppitt took off and immediately found the ailerons had switched to manual mode and locked in position. As a result he struggled to bring the aircraft into land. No reason for this incident was established despite tests carried out by Vickers Supermarine. According to the squadron's operations book 'a modified handle was fitted to the aileron manual selector making it easier to grasp in an emergency'.

A mix of F1 and F2 Swifts were flown. Squadron records show that in August 1954 three new Swifts arrived during the month, a Mk1 from West Raynham and two camouflaged Mk2s from South Marston. The latter two were probably the first F2s delivered on 30 August, WK221 and WK240. This mark was considerably more difficult to handle and the squadron records show that only experienced Swift pilots were permitted to fly the F2.

By as late as October 1954 there were no climb and range data available and the service squadron embarked on a programme of developing this information, which in normal circumstances should

F1s WK212, WK211 and WK205 of 56 Squadron during a sortie from Waterbeach on 11 March 1954. Although barely a month old in this picture, within a year WK205 was to become one of the first Swifts to be withdrawn from service. *(Crown Copyright, MoD. Courtesy of Air Historical Branch (RAF))*

have been created during prototype testing.

Serviceability was often very low, with rarely two aircraft available to fly at any one time and on three occasions in 1954 the fleet was grounded, for a total of eleven weeks, while modifications were installed. The first were made after Flying Officer Thornton was lost, when a positive manual selector was installed with a warning light along with a number of other changes. These factors combined with inexperienced pilots and poor weather resulted in only 1,086 sorties and 781.23 hours flown in the year. Several of those hours were flown demonstrating the new fighter at displays and fly-pasts sometimes with up to six aircraft in formation and including the annual Battle of Britain fly-past.

In addition to twelve Swifts the squadron continued to operate fourteen Meteor Mk8s which proved to be fifty per cent more serviceable than the Swift. Never having received their full complement of Swifts, the decision was taken that the F1 should not enter operational service and that the squadron was to re-equip fully with the Hawker Hunter Mk5 and the Swifts were retired on 15 March 1955, after only a little over twelve months service. Roy Rimington was airborne at the time the orders came through from the Secretary of State for Air and he completed the last training flight of a Swift at Waterbeach. The survivors were ferried to RAF Halton to be prepared as instructional airframes or to be scrapped.

Germany

Political conflict between the Western and Eastern power blocs had become heightened in the early 1950s as a result of the Korean War and coupled with the ongoing tensions around Berlin, the RAF was encouraged to upgrade its aerial reconnaissance capability. Gloster

Meteor FR9s and the unarmed FR10s replaced the Spitfires of II (AC) Squadron and 79 Squadron was re-formed at Gütersloh with Meteor FR9s. Technical developments were so rapid in the Jet Age that within five years it was clear that the Eastern Bloc air forces outmatched the Meteors. The MiG-15's success in Korea saw its wide deployment in Eastern Europe and the British could not field anything equivalent and so looked to the United States to fill the gap. The 2nd Tactical Air Force accordingly received the Canadian-built Sabre F4 which was the RAF's only first-line fighter until 1956, after which it was replaced by the Hawker Hunter that began to enter service in 1955. In the all-important reconnaissance role the Meteor PR10s were replaced by the English Electric Canberra and both II (AC) and 79 Squadrons were re-equipped with Swift FR5s.

By 1959 the RAF in Germany was concentrated around the Rhine with the day-fighter and fighter-reconnaissance squadrons based closer to the East German border at Jever and Gütersloh. These units were responsible for maintaining border integrity and in the view of commander-in-chief and the air officer commanding, Air Vice-Marshall William Crisham, 'the standards of aircrew were higher than ever before'. The problem was the number of experienced aircrew required was greater than available and in the case of the Swift fighter-reconnaissance pilots they had to be exceptionally experienced.

Flight magazine pointed out in their 28 August 1959 issue that the 2nd and 4th Allied Tactical Air Forces faced a formidable foe across the Air Defence Interception Zone. On the other side were around 1,200 aircraft of the air forces of East Germany, Poland, and Czechoslovakia, all backed up by the large aerial forces of the USSR.

Gütersloh with three Hawker Hunter day-fighter squadrons and Jever with two were each supported by their own fighter reconnaissance, Swift-equipped, squadrons. The Hunters were controlled from the sector operational centre at Brockzetel, using a Decca Type 80 radar managed from an extensive underground bunker. The Type 80 was a large radar installation providing early warning search facilities, which could distinguish two aircraft flying a mile apart over 150 miles away, representing three quarters of its 200-mile range. The reflector was seventy-five feet wide and twenty-five feet high which was slowly turned at four revolutions per minute by two to four 50 horsepower motors. The day-fighter squadrons were on a rota of week-long standby duties. During the duty, there were would be two aircraft on five-minute readiness, with another two on thirty minutes.

The Swifts of 79 Squadron at Gütersloh and of II (AC) Squadron at Jever, were controlled by the Tactical Operations Centre at Goch. Aircrew were mostly ex-instructors on second or third tours with the experience necessary to operate in a politically sensitive region, at very low-level altitudes and at high speed. Their area of responsibility covered six zones which they shared with the RAF Canberra photo-reconnaissance squadrons. Characteristically operating at 250 feet and below, the Swifts would also fly between zones at 500 feet and in inclement weather at 2,000 feet.

Flight described a typical mission where 79 Squadron was sent to photograph thirty bridges on which the army was practising demolition techniques and wanted to know the efficacy of their camouflage. It was a matter of pride with the FR5 pilots that they had developed a very high degree of familiarity of the border areas and would need fewer images and therefore less development time in the mobile photographic centres to produce the information requested.

Sylt

When occupied in 1945 the Sylt Luftwaffe base was renamed B170 Westerland and by September of that year it had been again renamed RAF Sylt. Located near the Danish border it became an armament practice station until it was handed back to the German military in October 1961. It was home to the 2nd Tactical Air Force Air-Sea Rescue Flight from February 1955 to September 1961. The ASR crews were a mix of German and British civilians who operated five German-built boats used for rescue and target towing duties.

NATO fighter squadrons were expected to spend at least a month a year at Sylt on live round gunnery practice on ranges over the North Sea. Resident squadrons, based at the north camp were tasked with target-towing duties flying a mix of Meteor F8s and T7s from the RAF and the Belgian air force. Targets were white nylon banners 30 ft long and 6 ft wide and would be towed over the measured range at 180 knots. A metal spreader bar was used for the radar to lock onto the target, typically at a range of 3,000 ft.

Kevin Hutchinson recalled that the visiting squadrons and the weapons training squadrons were based at the South Camp. A wide variety of aircraft flew into Sylt from Europe's air forces. The RAF squadrons were equipped with Hunters, Swifts, Meteor NF11s and

Javelins, the German air force with F-86 Sabres and F-84F Thunderstreaks, the navy with Hawker Sea Hawks and the Belgians with Meteors and Hunters.

Royal Flush

From the late 1950s to the very early 1970s NATO's various aerial reconnaissance competitions gave kudos to the winners, became part of the training curriculum but were also rather divisive. Only a very small number of crews from each unit could take part and naturally the better crews were selected to the detriment of the less capable. At certain times the 'winner takes all' philosophy precluded proper exchange of technology and ideas.

For those involved though competitions, such as Sassoon, Big Click and Royal Flush were useful, probably a great deal of fun and for the winners an important success. For the photographers and photo interpreters working in the field, these exercises were very important. The largest was the annual Royal Flush, where the best pilot was selected and the winning team awarded the Gruenther trophy for proficiency in photo-reconnaissance among Allied Air Forces Central Europe.

The trophy was made in England in 1955 and donated for the competition by the Republic Aviation Corporation. Named after General Alfred Maximilian Gruenther, a West Point graduate who became the youngest four-star general in the US Army's history. An academic with legendary analytical abilities he served as deputy chief of staff under General Eisenhower. Promoted to chief planner for the Allied invasion of North Africa, known as Operation Torch, and as chief of staff for General Mark Clark, he was vital to the plans to invade Italy and the subsequent push north.

He was appointed deputy commanding general of the US forces in Austria and in 1951, at the age of fifty-three was promoted to a four-star general. Post-war he was chief of staff at NATO headquarters and then commander of the Supreme Headquarters Allied Powers, Europe. He believed that due to its superior air power the West could defeat the Communist East but warned of a degradation in both quantity and quality of the Allied forces. Following his retirement in 1956 he became president of the American Red Cross, devoting his considerable skills to developing and promoting the organisation.

Formation of the 2nd Tactical Air Force photo-reconnaissance Royal Flush team. It consisted of a RAF Supermarine Swift (left), a Belgian air force RF-84F (top), a silver 306 Squadron (Royal Netherlands Air Force) RF-84F (below) and an RAF Canberra (right). *(Dutch Institute for Military History)*

1957

The second Royal Flush was held from 21 to 23 May 1957 at RAF Laarbruch in Germany. The contestants were the 2nd Allied Tactical Air Force made up of Dutch and Belgian RF-84Fs and RAF Canberra PR7s and Swift FR5s; and 1956 winners, the 4th Allied Tactical Air Force flying USAF Martin RB-57s and French air force RF-84Fs.

For the first day of the event the weather was very good but it progressively deteriorated to the point that it became a handicap to the teams. An indication of the intensity of the competition was that air traffic control managed to handle thirty-four movements of all types and sizes of aircraft over a one-and-a-half-hour period on the last day.

The Swifts and the Belgian RF-84F Thunderflashs used the same type of camera with two options – the four-inch which took a wider angle image and the eight-inch which was narrower and more detailed. During the competitions, the aircraft would taxi right up to the photographic trailers, allowing the technicians to swiftly unload the cameras and take them immediately to the large developing machines. The photographic interpreters only had thirty minutes between the shut-down of the aircraft engine to the

presentation of a report and substantiating prints.

The awards presentation, on Friday 24 May, held in 31 Squadron's No. 3 hangar was presided over by General Jean Etienne Valluy, commander-in-chief Allied Forces Central Europe and attended by 300 officers and men. Commander, Air Marshal the Earl of Bandon, welcomed fifty distinguished visitors, including twenty NATO generals to the event. Squadron Leader Wrigley accepted the Gruenther trophy on behalf of the winners, 2nd ATAF who scored 769½ points, while the 4th ATAF managed 575. In the low-level event, 79 Squadron was victorious and the Swift pilot Flight Lieutenant A. B. Laurence received an award donated by Vickers-Armstrongs. A 17 Squadron Canberra flown by Flying Officers H. G. Thompson and W. T. Bowden collected the high-level award. All air, ground, and photographic personnel received a plaque to mark the groups' successes.

The planned air display was cancelled due to the weather although a Hunter did perform a five-minute display. Interestingly, NATO's latest reconnaissance aircraft, the Vickers Valiant Douglas RB66 Destroyer, were on static display alongside the latest photographic equipment.

1958

Spangdahlem hosted Royal Flush III, between 24 August and 12 September 1958. Again the 2nd ATAF won the trophy, but this time

TOP TO BOTTOM
42 Squadron Republic RF-84F Thunderflash FR-11/H8-L taxiing out of Lahr air base during the 1956 Royal Flush exercise. In the foreground is Swift FR5 WK287 'A' of II (AC) Squadron then based at Geilenkirchen. *(Jacques Schelfaut)* Winners of the 1957 Royal Flush competition low-level event, with the winning pilot, Flight Lieutenant Laurence, on the far left. *(Solent Sky Museum)*

Members of the winning team and Swift FR5 WK309 of the 1958 NATO Tactical Reconnaissance Competition, Royal Flush, in which the Swift FR5 was the only aircraft able to find its target by winding its way down a cloud-covered valley in the German Sauerland. (*Nigel Walpole*)

the high-level competition was won by a 31 Squadron crew, Flying Officers P. T. Taylor and A. T. Burt in a Canberra, and French air force pilots, Lieutenants A. Brun and D. E. Saget, flying RF-84Fs took first and second place respectively in the low-level section.

The scores were also somewhat higher with the 2nd ATAF being awarded 11,916 points and the 4th ATAF 11,218. What was significant was that retired General Gruenther, presented the Gruenther trophy to the 2nd ATAF representative Wing Commander A. A. J. Sanders.

1959

For the third year in a row the 2nd ATAF were presented the Gruenther trophy, this time by Prince Bernhard of the Netherlands. Held at the Royal Netherlands Air Force Eindhoven base on 2 and 3 June, thirty-two sorties were flown against eighty targets and the two team's scores were 10,645 for 2nd ATAF and 9,435 for 4th ATAF. The winners only missed one target while their rivals missed seven overall.

British, Dutch and Belgian teams of the 2nd ATAF flew the Canberra at high level and the Swift FR5 and RF-84F at low level while the 4th ATAF was made up of a French air force team flying RF-84Fs and three American teams, two equipped with the RB-66s and one introducing for the first time the RF-101 Voodoos. Two NATO air forces were excluded from the competitions; the Royal Canadian Air Force, which had no reconnaissance units in Europe and the West German air force which was still in the process of re-equipping.

Speed was measured as time from chocks away, flight time and speed of the development of photographic evidence but this only accounted for thirty per cent of the marks per flight. Not surprisingly accuracy of information was what really determined the winners. *Flight* magazine reported that an RAF Canberra started rolling twenty-nine seconds after its crew had left the briefing and a USAF Voodoo took thirty-four minutes to reach a target on the Suffolk coast, take the necessary photographs and return to Eindhoven.

Weather for the competition was ideal and there were good results due to strong crews supported by efficient ground crew and the skilled work of the photographic sections of each team. The Swifts flown by Flight Lieutenants Alexander McLean Cobban and J. H. Turner of 79 Squadron were judged as the best team and Flying Officer B. Stead of 80 Squadron in a Canberra, the best individual pilot.

The Royal Flush competitions were initially held at a single base and this was followed by six years where the participants operated from their home bases, with the final at a selected base. Then the system reverted to being held at a host base. From 1978 the Royal Flush was merged with the Tactical Weapons Meet and became the NATO Tactical Air Meet.

II (AC) Squadron

Number II (Army Cooperation) Squadron, known as 'Shiny Two', was founded on 13 May 1912 at Farnborough and was one of the founding members of the Royal Flying Corps (RFC).

It quickly gained a pioneering reputation as it set the British altitude record of 16,000 ft in August 1913 and in August 1914, deployed the first British fixed-wing aircraft to fight in a war when the squadron deployed to France. After the Second World War, the squadron moved to Germany where it spent forty-seven years before moving to RAF Marham with the Tornado GR1A. The years in Germany saw II (AC) Squadron operate Swifts, Hunters, Phantoms and Jaguars.

Under Squadron Leader Ron Mortley AFC the 'Shiny Two' became the first RAF squadron to be equipped with a jet fitted with an afterburner. The first Swift FR5 arrived at Geilenkirchen on 24 February 1956 replacing the Meteor FR9. Pilot Eric Sharp said, 'it was a lovely aircraft at 420 knots and at low level. It was stable and if a map was dropped on the cockpit floor the pilot could lean down to retrieve it and the aircraft would remain rock steady.'

Fitted with power controls and a manual option, Eric remarked that when the power controls were engaged on the ground it was possible to experience a 'false lock'. This was when it appeared the powered option had been selected but if the locking pins were not opposite their slots in the piston rod, the hydraulic pressure would lock on the pins. Any moderate load would release the lock and the controls would then be very heavy and often it was difficult to change to the powered option.

They flew with the 250-gallon ventral tank which did affect the speed of the aircraft, but without this tank there was only a very limited flight endurance. The flaps acted as an airbrake and were fitted with a limiter when used as a brake to prevent damage. However, pilots had to be very aware not to confuse the flap limiter with the brake booster when on finals to land. This would result in limited flap extension and locked wheels on landing. As happened to XD950 in April 1959 when both main wheels burst and the aircraft ran off on to the grass closing the runway for several hours.

Alan Middleton was with the 'Shiny Two' from January 1954 to January 1957 and the last ten months were on the Swift FR5. He recalls that the serviceability was low and that he only managed to amass 74.40 hours, which he said was 'as good as it went in those

A pair of FR5s being refuelled and prepared for the next sortie. *(Ron Mortley)*;
II (AC) Squadron's formal photograph in front of a Swift FR5 at Geilenkirchen on 28 April 1956. Back row (left to right): Mike Webb, Ken Pinder, Alan Middleton, Ross Colwill, John Whittam, Tighe Retief, Manx Kelly. Front row (left to right): Geoff Marlow, Dicky Green, Paddy King, CO Sqn Ldr Ron Mortley and squadron mascot 'Hereward' at his feet, Ray Bannard, Tony Winship and Pete Bulford. *(Squadron Leader Ron Mortley via his daughter Jill)*

days'. Like all the pilots he remembers the Swift as very strong and solid although with inferior performance and handling at height. He managed to reach 50,000 ft and found that in a turn the aircraft 'did a lazy sideslip round, and cost about 5,000 ft through 360 degrees'. This he found was disappointing when it was possible to outclimb the Hunter Mk4s.

The first major incident with a Swift occurred nearly a year after they entered service with the squadron. Flying Officer John Whittam was at 23,000 ft on 30 January 1957, when the engine flamed out. He made three attempts to relight it but failed and decided to carry out a dead stick landing. Landing downwind, he broke cloud to find himself thirty degrees off the runway. Under the controller's advice he aimed for the perimeter track. With no power and no hydraulics, the undercarriage would not lower and he struggled to activate the emergency lowering mechanism, obtaining three greens at the very last minute. Without the benefit of flaps, it was a high-speed touchdown, but Whittam's skill meant that there was no damage and he was awarded a green endorsement.

In the month that the squadron achieved their second place at Royal Flush II, Flight Lieutenant Lou Cockerill found himself on 21 May 1957 in a similar predicament to Whittam, when he lost his engine at 2,000 ft at a speed of 350 knots. He forced-landed XD924 on the main runway with no flaps and the undercarriage retracted. A testimony to the renowned strength of the Swift was that it only sustained Cat 3 damage and Cockerill was awarded a green endorsement. The aircraft was repaired and suffered further Cat 3 damage in July 1958 and May 1959, before it was stuck off charge, after a final accident in August 1960.

Two months later, on 8 July, XD912 flamed out at 3,000 ft when the fuel gauge showed 500 lbs still available. The pilot elected to undertake a straight-in flame-out approach, landed at 200 knots and applied 800 lbs of brake pressure saving the aircraft from running off the end of the runway. It was found that there was a failure of the fuel transfer pump but the gauges only measured the inner tanks, the only indication of a problem was the tail-heavy attitude as the fuel failed to transfer forwards. As a result, new orders were issued, instructing pilots to return to base when they had 800 lbs indicated as remaining.

Swift F4 WK277 was delivered to the RAF in April 1956 and then upgraded to FR5 standard in 1959 and issued to II (AC) Squadron as 'N'. Allocated as a ground trainer and coded 7719M. It is currently on display at the Newark Air Museum.
(*II (AC) Squadron*)

Flying in December 1957 was restricted by the poor weather and fog with most sorties flown at low level and serviceability issues hampered an Exercise Full House. These exercises were sprung on the squadron at any time, often once a month and sometimes more. They were fully operational exercises designed to simulate a real situation where an attack had taken place and the reconnaissance squadrons were tasked with gathering as much data as possible.

A move 200 miles north to Jever was made in January 1958 and despite the bad weather numerous trips were made to deliver ventral tanks ahead of the relocation. An advanced party left on 5 January and the main ground party completed the move on 15 January. Only two days flying was possible for the rest of that month due to persistent snow, ice, and fog.

The weather continued to affect flying in February and the sanding of runways to prevent slippages resulted in two, two-wheel landings caused by sand jamming the wheel locks in the up position. Despite this, work continued. Flight Lieutenants Whittam and Boyer flew to Sylt to carry out gun trials in an attempt to identify the cause of high stoppage rates. A Full House exercise was carried out but unusually over two days due to the inclement weather conditions.

Flying in April 1958 was concentrated on preparing for the Sylt camp and a Meteor 8 was used to tow a target ahead of the month away. Squadron Leader Ron Mortley was promoted and left the squadron, his replacement being Squadron Leader Chris Wade. Total hours flown was 207.50 over 268 sorties.

An example of the pioneering nature of flying the early jets was Flying Officer Danny Lavender's experience on 22 May 1958. Shortly after he had taken off in XD929, he was informed that there was a small amount of fuel venting from his aircraft. As it happened, the air-to-air gunnery practice was cancelled and the two Swifts had to burn off their fuel load before returning to base. In an unexpectedly short space of time Lavender found he was running short of fuel. He adopted a flame-out approach, used the emergency procedures to lower the undercarriage, but was only able to get twenty degrees of flap. As a result, he landed fast and flamed out the engine to help bring the Swift to a halt. The subsequent investigation showed that, on take-off and retraction of the undercarriage, the spinning wheel had chafed the fuel pipe which had caused the observed venting. Flying orders were again updated, requiring that the fuel pipes in the wheel wells were checked as part of the pre-flight walk around, and that brakes were applied prior to the undercarriage being retracted.

In one of the continual exercises the squadron took part in, two aircraft were sent to Karup in Denmark in exchange for two Danish air force RF-84Fs. The II (AC) Squadron aircraft then joined Jever's Hunters in a practice alert called by 2nd Allied Tactical Air Force Headquarters with the Swifts flying fighter-reconnaissance sorties against pre-planned targets and the Hunters providing defensive cover.

In one of the Sylt camps Flight Lieutenant Bernard St. Aubyn ejected from Swift XD928 several miles out to sea while returning from an air-to-air firing exercise off Sylt. The aircraft fortuitously crashed onto Rantum Beach, West Germany throwing wreckage against the cliff. It is reported that if the aircraft had been a hundred feet higher there was a possibility it would have crashed into the houses of Rantum. Unable to extricate himself from his 'chute shroud lines, a rescue helicopter towed St. Aubyn ashore. Kevin Hutchinson wrote:

> 'As a member of the crash crew I attended the scene an hour or so later, and was interested to see the Aden gun cradles visibly and audibly sizzling as the salt attacked the magnesium-aluminium alloy. Some months later the seat was washed up on the beach at Wenningsted, and, on his next visit to Sylt, Flight Lieutenant Bernard St. Aubyn was presented with part of the ejection gun in a small ceremony at the Station Armoury.'

A party of forty British schoolmasters visited RAF Jever from 11 to 12 May 1959. They arrived in the late afternoon where they were met by several officers from each squadron on the base and then escorted to the mess. After tea, they had a tour of the base and visited each squadron at their hangars. No. 4 Squadron conducted a demonstration of a scramble to end the day. Early the following morning there was a full flying programme. This began with the firing of a flare gun by one of the visitors and fifteen aircraft, five from each squadron, started their engines simultaneously. Displays were performed by a Chipmunk, Vampire and a Swift with a mass fly-past of the fifteen aircraft. Within an hour-and-a-half, it was all over and the teachers had left by ten o'clock.

Comet C Mk2 XK695, that brought a party of UK teachers for a visit to RAF Jever, is parked beside II (AC) Squadron's FR5s. The forward section of XK695 is on display at the de Havilland Aircraft Museum. *(Michael Ryan)*

Although published in *Swift Justice*, the following experience was related directly to the author by Roy Rimington. On 27 August 1959 Roy decided to set up a picture for that year's squadron Christmas card. He recalls:

'At the southern end of the north German plain are two hill ranges, the Wiehengebirge and the Wesergebirge which almost meet at Porta Westfalica through which the River Weser flows. This was a popular landmark for low-level fliers and commonly known as the Minden Gap after the large town which could clearly be seen through the hills to the northern side. On the eastern end of the western ridge, the Wiehengebirge, is a large statue of Kaiser Wilhelm which was erected in 1896 on the Wittekindsberg. Being 88 metres high it was also a popular landmark and much photographed by reconnaissance pilots. I often thought this would make a nice backdrop for the squadron Christmas card and decided to take a pair of Swifts on a training sortie and photograph the monument on the way back to Jever with a Swift in the foreground. Furthermore, I thought it would enhance the photograph if the Swift was straight and level inverted.

'I took Taffy Wallis with me as number two to take the photograph and briefed him to do a couple of practice passes on the way back to get his positioning right for photographing. We set out on a beautiful day in August, which happened to be my twenty-eighth birthday, to recce a couple of targets in the Harz mountains. On the way back I inverted for about ten seconds a couple of times for Taffy to practise the positioning. Then, when we were still about twenty miles south of the Minden Gap with excellent visibility I told Taffy we would make one more practice run before the final photographing over the target. He got into position with the right amount of overtaking speed and I inverted at about 300 knots. I was only inverted for a second or two when the RPM went down very rapidly with a sudden loss of power. I immediately rolled the right way up and climbed. The hydraulic reservoir had not emptied so I still had power control for a few seconds. It was immediately clear that the terrain ruled out a forced landing so I told Taffy that I was ejecting. I was then at about 800 ft. The canopy released cleanly and I pulled the face blind which was the only means of ejection with the Mk2 seat.

'The first thing I remember following the ejection, in which I obviously blacked out, was a tremendous wrench on my left leg as the parachute opened. I realised that I was hanging upside-down with the parachute harness flailing freely about ten feet above me with one buckle caught in the crotch loop holding my left thigh. My first thought was how to reach the lift webs to guide myself away from the river rushing up towards me. Fortunately, I had no way of avoiding a ducking and went head first into the middle of the River Weser. I just had time to inflate the Mae West and as soon as I hit the water the parachute harness came free as the friction was released between the straps. I entered the river about five miles south of Hamelin (Hamelin of Pied Piper fame) and here it is about 50 yards wide at the most. I soon reflected that the river probably saved my life or at least very serious injury.

'By the time I had reached the east bank of the river a British Army Land Rover had appeared with three or four soldiers. They were extremely helpful and lent me dry

II Squadron aircrew photograph taken between 1 January and 22 March 1960. Back row (from left to right): Roy Rimington, Pete Adair, Al Newing, Derek Burton, Maurice Dale, Taff Wallis, John Watson, Eric Sharp and Philip Holden-Rushworth. Front row (from left to right): Bunny St Aubyn, Dave Ives, Al Ibbett, Boss Chris Wade, Olaf Bergh, Al Martin and Derek Gathercole. *(Thanks to Phil Holden-Rushworth)*

clothing, but were very anxious to go off and find the other pilot they had seen. It took me a while to reassure them that I was alone and it was probably the ejection seat they had seen falling away. They then drove me to Rinteln Army Hospital since my back was rather painful and I suspected some injury. However, following an X-ray and examination by an army doctor it was considered to be mere bruising. By this time a helicopter had been launched from Detmold to pick me up from Rinteln and I thanked the soldiers after obtaining their names and unit so I could return the clothes. On our journey from Rinteln to Detmold the helicopter pilot found the remains of the Swift which fortunately had not caused any damage on the ground. Following a pleasant lunch in the officers' mess, much to the concern of some members since I appeared as a very untidy and incorrectly dressed private soldier, I was flown from Detmold to Jever in a Beaver.'

About six months later Roy visited the doctor after he suffered pain in his back, caused he thought by skiing. The X-rays showed that his back had healed well following a fracture. In the ejection, it was found that he had suffered a compression fracture of the spine and three vertebrae were fused together!

TOP TO BOTTOM
FR5 WK289/V of II (AC)
Squadron at Biggin Hill on 17
September 1960 immediately
prior to transfer to 79 Squadron.
(Jerry Hughes);
In flight over a wooded German
countryside, FR5 XD962/J was
originally allocated to 79
Squadron but was then allocated
to II (AC) Squadron and arrived
on 10 August 1960. Less than a
year later it was flown to 60
Maintenance Unit on 22 March
1961 and allocated to the fire
dump at RAF Bovingdon. It was
only scrapped in 1976.
(John Mackenzie)

Roy again:

'This was not the first time a parachute harness
had released on ejection. This had happened
when a pilot was ejected unintentionally from a
Javelin at 35,000 ft. His harness also fell away
on seat separation at 10,000 ft but he fortunately held on to one strap and descended with
one arm hooked through the leg loop. Tests
were carried out on some parachute harnesses
and it was found that a sharp blow with a metal
object on the harness box, even with the safety
pin inserted, could release the spring-loaded
catches and the harness straps under tension
would fly free. It was therefore surmised that if
the metal seat harness box was on top of the
metal parachute harness box, the G force of
ejection in the Mk2 seat was sufficient to
depress the catches and release the parachute
harness. From then on instructions were issued
to keep the two harness boxes apart with the
parachute box as high as possible and the seat harness box
low with the thigh straps as tight as possible.'

On Monday 26 October 1959, Al Martin was forced to eject for a
second time in his career, when the engine of WK304 failed over the
North Sea. He had made every effort to return to Jever, gliding over
Wilhelmshaven toward Roffhausen. Fast losing height and faced with
the prospect that if he left the aircraft if could plough into the
Olympia Werks, where thousands of employees were at work, he
ejected very late. The aircraft crashed 300 metres from the factory,
and the blazing cockpit slid across the main road. Martin suffered
cuts and bruises and a back injury as there had been no time for the
parachute to fully deploy. The end of the year was focused on training
for Royal Flush VI, in between the three Full House exercises which
were conducted using the Royal Flush flight profiles and techniques.

The last new Swift had been delivered to II (AC) Squadron in
August 1960 and within six months the squadron began to prepare for
re-equipment with the Hawker Hunter FR10. During January 1961,
the remaining six Swifts flew 185 hours and the eight new Hunters

managed 92 hours. Having the Hunters available proved to be a useful training and cross-over aid for the technical and logistics teams to develop their knowledge on the new aircraft. The Swifts had become increasingly difficult to maintain due to a shortage of spares and their imminent withdrawal. The last Swift left Jever on 13 May 1961. After conversion to the Hunter FR10, II (AC) Squadron moved to Gütersloh.

79 Squadron RAF

The squadron was formed at Gosport on 1 August 1917 and moved to France three months later, spending the duration of the First World War carrying out fighter patrols and ground-attack missions. In a role that was to be repeated, the squadron remained in Germany as part of the occupying forces until it was disbanded in July 1919. Reformed in March 1937 at Biggin Hill, the squadron saw service in the Battle of Britain and the Far East, and was again disbanded on 30 December 1945. It was reformed in November 1951 at Gütersloh, in the North Rhine Westphalia region of Germany.

Built as part of the rearmament programme, Gütersloh opened as a Luftwaffe base in April 1937. Units based there took part in the invasion of Poland and the Netherlands and then from 1941 to 1944 it served as a maintenance centre for night fighters. As the Allied forces drew closer it became a fully operational night-fighter station and in the last stages of the war the airfield was used for Messerschmitt Me 262 jet-fighter operations.

Captured by the Americans in April 1945 it was handed over to the British occupying forces, which used the town as the RAF No. 2 Group Headquarters and initially based three squadrons of de Havilland Mosquito FB6s at the airfield. Various units and aircraft types had operated out of Gütersloh before 79 Squadron was formed there and equipped with Gloster Meteor FR9s. With the arrival in April 1952 of 541 Squadron and a month later II (AC) Squadron flying Meteor PR10s and FR9s respectively, the base was largely focused on aerial reconnaissance until October 1954 when it became a bomber base for RAF squadrons flying the English Electric Canberra B2.

It reverted to the reconnaissance role in September 1956 with the arrival of 79 Squadron equipped with Supermarine Swift FR5s. When the Swifts were withdrawn, Hawker Hunter FR10 tactical

OPPOSITE, TOP TO BOTTOM
XD925 was an unusual visitor to hangar 5 at RAF Gütersloh, which was the home of the Canberra squadron, the engine and wing of one slightly in view. It is believed it was there for refuelling.
(*Barry Flahey*);
Swift FR5 WK281 was delivered to the RAF in late 1956 and served with 79 Squadron, passing on to 4 Squadron for a short time until assigned to 60 Maintenance Unit at RAF Church Fenton in 1961. Withdrawn from use, it went to 14 ATC Squadron at RAF Uxbridge until it was allocated for ground training at RAF Colerne in March 1967 and given the serial number 7112M. It is currently on display at the Tangmere Museum. It is pictured here at the RAF 50th Anniversary air show at RAF Abingdon on 15 June 1968.
(*Dave Welch*)

reconnaissance aircraft operated from the airfield until 1971. Situated east of the Rhine and within minutes of the East German border it was developed in the mid-1960s, as a principal air defence base and home to English Electric Lightning F2s. Later Hawker Siddeley Harrier squadrons took on the dual roles of ground support and reconnaissance. Westland Puma HC1 helicopters, Boeing Chinook HC1 helicopters and Rapier missiles provided support, logistics and defence until 1993 when the RAF withdrew and Gütersloh became the Princess Royal Barracks, Gütersloh, a British Army helicopter base, where they remained until September 2016.

79 Squadron excelled at the Royal Flush competition and held the Sassoon trophy awarded annually for photo-reconnaissance efficiency. The Meteors would normally operate in pairs but this practice changed to single aircraft sorties on the Swift as there were insufficient aircraft available and overall serviceability was generally poor. This was a result of the extra complexities in the more modern jet, the lack of availability of spares from central stores and the fact that there were too few Swifts on station to allow for maintenance schedules and breakdowns to maintain the necessary readiness levels. It was very different with the Hunter squadrons. Although they suffered engine flame outs and were restricted to only firing two guns together and there was a tendency for the cartridge links to be ingested, there were always aircraft available on the flight line as there were sufficient to be properly cycled through the well provisioned repair and maintenance facilities.

Gütersloh was fitted with nylon crash barriers at either end of the runway, which could be raised from the control tower. Supplied by a Swedish company they were designed to prevent uncontrolled run-offs from the runway in the event of flap or brake failure on landing. A barrier was known on one occasion to have caused a problem on take-off when it was inadvertently left in the up position and the approaching Swift just managed to skim over the top.

When Ian Waller joined 79 Squadron he initially flew the Gloster Meteor FR9 and then from August 1956 until November 1957 the Swift FR5. He enjoyed the robustness of the Swift and feeling of control at low level and high speed. The aircraft was very strongly built and could take the extreme buffeting from air movement and disturbances over ground objects and the terrain. At the start, there were no height restrictions, but in time the official minimum height was 250 feet. It was largely ignored and continual practice at very low levels honed the skills of the RAF pilots in low-level reconnaissance. To be effective in this environment Ian noted that it was important to mark vital points on a route for every thirty seconds or minute of the flight, 'as travelling at seven miles per minute you would only have time to glance at the map finding the clearly marked points, there was not time to study the map'.

Commenting on the general characteristics of the Swift, Ian remarked:

> 'If control was lost at sufficient height, certainly above 15,000 ft, a pilot could take their hands off the controls and the aircraft would recover, any lower it was advisable to eject. There was a tendency for the aircraft to drop its left wing when becoming supersonic in a dive and to recover from the dive the VI tail was used to disturb the airflow over the tail plane sufficiently to return control. It also proved to be a reasonably good gun platform. Fitted with two cannon with 180 rounds a side, but usually only carried 100 rounds for practice firing, making it easy to count per cent strikes. There were no missiles and the pilot had to work out the deflection as the gun sight was useless at low level. The speed and proximity to the ground made it essential that the pilot maintained a sharp awareness of what was happening outside the aircraft. Lining up a fleeting target through the site narrowed the pilot's field of vision and vital seconds would be lost assimilating what had changed while the pilot was focused on the sight.'

Reconnaissance aircraft of the United States forces were fitted with camera sighting scopes but the RAF Swift pilots were not even provided with guidance marks on the canopies. Nigel Walpole recounted how accuracy over the target was down to experience, which was very quickly gained. He did emphasise that in his opinion the pilot's observations were highly important in providing immediate situation reports back to the command centre. Reliance solely on the images would mean often vital information would have to wait for the return flight and then processing of the photographs, by which time conditions on the ground could very well have changed. The army needed to know what was directly ahead, which routes were being used by the advancing forces, what the strength of those forces were and if the roads and bridges they were on were usable. There was rarely an opportunity to go around again and typically Nigel said they would be travelling at speeds between 480 to 560 knots, or if they were short of fuel 420 knots. Sometimes they would arrive over the co-ordinates given for the sortie and it was not clear what they were looking for and they would report 'nothing seen at location given'. By the 1960s Nigel feels that there was a lot more discipline around speed and height than in the 1950s, but there was less of a buccaneer spirit.

Ian Waller noted that tests performed at various heights and speeds, showed that the optimum combination for stable flight was found to be below 50 ft at a speed of 420 knots. A typical mission profile was to maintain these low altitudes inbound to the target, which were below the radar scans and the only threat at that height in those days was from small-arms fire. The pilot would aim to arrive over the threshold of the target at below 50 ft and would then fly a banana pattern up to 300 ft, with a fifty-degree bank. Although this blocked off one camera the other side and nose target facing oblique cameras could obtain the best images, while permitting the pilot to observe other features and equipment on the airfield.

The return leg followed a different route, during which the task was to carry out a 'lines of communication search'. The purpose of which was to observe railway lines, roads, and canals for the movement of troops and equipment. If anything important was seen the pilot would climb to 4,000 ft and report the position with a Flash call and a box of four-rocket-equipped Venoms would be called onto the target. The danger of doing this is that the previously 'hidden' Swift would immediately be 'painted' by radar.

A primary task was to carry out airfield reconnaissance and Exercise Guest was an important element of the readiness training.

Seen at Biggin Hill on 19 September 1959 is FR5 XD974/M of 79 Squadron. A year later it was written off due to maintenance issues , possibly as it had been used as a spares ship.
(Jerry Hughes)

This was called once a month without warning and was expected to simulate a real-life war situation. The pattern was to take off in the dark and arrive over the target at first light. Of course, this suited the pilots and ground crew in winter when dawn was around 0800 hrs but it was very different in summer when take-off was required at 0230 hrs. To facilitate these exercises, targets in West Germany were identified that could closely resemble the actual target, with the emphasis being placed on similar landmarks, such as crossroads, a canal or railway. Ian noted that his target was Magdeburg airfield in East Germany, while his practice target was near Koblenz. Other missions carried out were air-to-air and air-to-ground training in reconnaissance and live gunnery, often as with II (AC) Squadron at RAF Sylt.

While flying XD923 at 100 ft, at a speed of 580 knots Ian Waller found the aircraft swung 30 degrees and then like a pendulum, back through the centre line 30 degrees the other way. Ian thought this was strange and on landing he enquired as to whom was next rostered to fly XD923. Discovering that an inexperienced newer pilot had been assigned to the aircraft, he suggested that someone with more Swift experience would be more suitable. Shortly after he was summoned out to the flight line and shown that the fillet between the wing and the fuselage was missing; which explained the wild pendulum movement at speed.

John Sawyer joined the RAF as a Boy Entrant in 1956. He was trained at RAF St Athan, and after his first posting to RAF Waterbeach, he was allocated to a fitters' course at RAF Weeton, and then back to 63 Squadron, before being sent on a tour with 2TAF, on 79 Squadron at RAF Gütersloh and Jever. He arrived in

Germany in October of 1959, to find that there were no Swift-type courses, and the only introduction to the aircraft was a handout, and a walk round with an NCO.

John remembers that the aircraft was prone to fuel leaks from the wing tanks.

> 'Requirements to maintain serviceability often resulted in rushing the procedures used to cure the sealant. As this cure time was temperature critical, petrol-fired heaters were used to raise the internal tank temperature, but German winters and open hangar doors made the process very difficult and the end result somewhat unpredictable.'

Problems caused by hydraulic failure, often required the removal of the engine. Three large panels on top of the fuselage had to be removed and the engine was lifted out at an angle, being inched back slowly to clear the fin. John became an expert at this and controlled the overhead crane, positioned in the hangar roof with the operator in a small cabin 75 ft above the hangar floor. During Royal Flush in the French Zone John carried out an engine change away from base, using a jib crane, that involved a demonstration of skill by a German driver, using a crane that was twice the size of the aircraft.

The engines required removal and maintenance every 400 hours. The Avon 100 series suffered from problems with the pressure variable ram and fuel pump. During John's time with 79 Squadron there were three engine failures which resulted in ejections. He also noted that there were four bird strikes, and that it was a very unpleasant job to remove an engine that had suffered one.

Radio and electronic problems were fairly few as the kit was very basic. The IFF (identification friend or foe) aerial was mounted on top of the fin and its cable ran under the engine to the cockpit. It was not impervious to hydraulic fluid and there was often lots of that lying in the engine bay; any IFF breakdowns meant a full engine removal.

Because the supply chain was long and slow, it was common practice to find a suitable donor aircraft to provide an instant fix. Eventually this donor would be stripped of all useful parts. Supermarine specific screws and anchor nuts were not easy to obtain. Some were the same as those used on the Hunter, but it would have been illegal to use these on the Swift which forced the ground crew to make use of contacts in other squadrons to provide the necessary Hunter spares for use on the Swift. With parts, totally unique to the Swift such subterfuge was not an option. The anchor nuts to fasten the engine covers were in high demand and difficult to source. John wrote that he suspected that the aircraft 'should have been stress jacked for engine removal, but generally they were not, so refitting these was a problem on some aircraft, causing cross threaded screws and the eventual failure of the fastener, and we could not get replacements'. Often the crews would use glue which would require them to drill out the offending screw the next time the engine was removed.

There were difficulties where aircraft were not built to the same standard, such as at least three F4s that were converted to FR5s. John mentioned the rear tank low pressure switch as a perfect example.

> 'This was accessed on all of them through a panel on the lower port side rear, via a hole just big enough to take an arm. The switch was higher than your head, and retained by a 3/8th banjo bolt, which had a bonded seal top and bottom. Wirelocked, naturally. This was bad enough on the ones that you could reach as a one-handed exercise, with about five gallons of fuel trickling down your arm and ending up around your knees, as this was a kneeling job, under the rear fuselage. On some aircraft, this was a fingertip job and could take several hours, or less on other aircraft and a mere ten minutes on the bench without the fuselage getting in the way. It meant manipulating a 3/8th x 5/16 spanner one handed, fitting the banjo bolt and its top and bottom bonded seals, then wire locking, and finishing off with pliers. There was also the electrical connection, which involved two 6 BA screws and the use of a watchmaker's screwdriver on the cover plate plus two 2 BA nuts inside and manipulation of a 2 BA spanner. All of these tools were tied to a piece of string to aid recovery in the event of their being dropped, which happened often.'

Towards the end of the service life of the aircraft it was found that the main plane retaining bolts and bushes were wearing as a result of the stresses of the continual buffeting and high G manoeuvres experienced in their low-level role, and a programme was initiated to remove and replace these on the entire fleet. This often meant that four aircraft from 2 and 79 Squadrons were out of use for some six weeks at a time, which added to the pressure of maintaining the few serviceable aircraft available.

Morale was a big problem for the squadron. Ground crews felt removed from the operation and it was only later that they were privy to the magnificent pictures being taken by their aircraft. The images were displayed in the crew room with details of the pilot, height, and speed; all the information the fairly keen airmen wanted. There were accounts of unfair charges being laid and poor man management which resulted in some 'work to rule' actions, which affected the serviceability of the aircraft. The crews worked to the book and insisted on correct working practices which inevitably slowed down aircraft turn around. There was a great deal of pressure to provide aircraft without the proper resources to hand. Many airmen did cut corners to achieve the required serviceability. As John stated 'this did not mean that the aircraft were in any way not airworthy, but they were carrying a lot of snags which on a normal squadron would not be allowed, and one of us had to sign these off. Refusing to sign was one of our last resorts.'

John concludes: 'I liked the airframe and its engine for the sheer brute power that we felt when running it. It was a challenging aircraft.'

There were eleven major incidents with 79 Squadron's Swifts, four of them due to engine failure, with the second most common fault being with the undercarriage. There were also flying accidents and one demonstrates the strength of the Swift. Nigel Walpole provides a detailed account in *Swift Justice,*

An unidentified ex-79 Squadron FR5 at 71 Maintenance Unit at RAF Bicester. *(Tim Wood)*

which is summarised here. Flying WK278 Flight Lieutenant Pat King was on an exercise to find a target about the size of a phone box and was under pressure to adhere to the expected flight time, irrespective of difficulties that may arise. The weather was closing in which caused Pat to increase speed to the search area to allow some time to slow down and locate the target. He recalls how 'soon I was flying very low and at 360 knots below the cloud, having selected half flap to increase manoeuvrability and keeping a sharp eye open for electrical pylons and radio masts'. Despite a worsening situation and against better judgement he continued until the conditions became so poor that he was forced to abort the mission. Mistaking his position, he elected to stay below the main cloud, but in a few seconds, he saw the rapid approach of a forest of pine trees. Risking a high-speed stall, he pulled back hard on the stick and as he did so the underside of the aircraft impacted with the tops of the trees with a fearful noise. Knowing that he had damaged the aircraft but not to what extent, he gingerly gained height and made for base. Arriving overhead he requested a flyby inspection, tested the handling in landing configuration and then successfully put the battered aircraft on the ground. The underside was extensively damaged, to the extent that, together with the imminent withdrawal of the Swifts, the decision was taken to scrap WK278.

To quote Pat King, 'I certainly recall the sturdy Swift because its robustness saved my life. If I had been in any other fighter aircraft of the time I am quite certain that I would on that day have made a contribution, albeit minor, to organic pine tree growing in the Federal Republic of Germany. The Swift and 17 November 1960, I remember well.'

The squadron was disbanded at Jever on 30 December 1960, but almost immediately reformed as IV (AC) Squadron on 1 January 1961. Initially equipped with Swift FR5s, a legacy from 79 Squadron, these were soon replaced by Hawker Hunter FR.10s. The last Swift was returned to the UK on 7 March 1961 when it was repositioned from Gütersloh to Church Fenton. A total of ninety-four FR5s had seen service with the RAF.

CHAPTER 7

WK275 – The last F4

OPPOSITE TOP
Probably late 1950s or early 1960s,
WK275 looks in very good
condition and very modern, in
sharp contrast to the pre-war car
in the background. *(via Tim Wood)*

BELOW
Peter Thorne's logbook recording
his flights in WK275 on 30 June
1953, where he was assessing the
flying tail. *(Air Cdre Peter Thorne)*

WK275 IS THE ONLY F4 remaining. Its history and restoration
covers its operational life as a test and development airframe and
the part it played in bringing into service facilities that today are
considered as normal in many combat aircraft.

The service life of WK275 is very difficult to track down. It only
flew on average five hours a month from delivery to the RAF on 28
March 1955 through to July 1957. Two of those flights were by Peter
Thorne on 16 and 19 August 1955 when he carried out an assess-
ment of the variable incidence tail plane. Fitted with the all flying
tail plane with tabs it was the first Swift reported to
have excellent handling.

This configuration provided far greater control at
the higher Mach numbers where the normal fixed
horizontal stabiliser and elevator was prone to a lack
of control. This is because the break between the two
elements creates a disturbance in the airflow and
series of shocks and instability. The all flying tail plane
produces less drag, requires less control force, and
provides a larger surface with which to manage airflow.
It provides stability during transition from subsonic to
supersonic flight and overcomes the blanking of the
tail plane experienced during transonic flight and the
loss of the effectiveness of the elevators. Its prime
purpose is to exert enormous control forces in the
pitch axis at crucial points in the flight envelope.

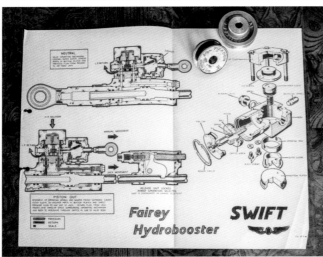

Hydrobooster units were fitted which controlled the flight surfaces, ailerons and the variable incidence tail plane, hydraulically rather than manually. *(Tim Wood);* The tail planes from WK275 stripped of paint show the variable incidence surfaces with no elevators. *(Jet Art Aviation)*

Chris Wilson, of Jet Art Aviation describes the variable incidence tail plane fitted to WK275.

'It consists of a single piece aerofoil wing structure fitted to each side of the aircraft's rear fuselage. Each tail plane is mounted onto a spigot that protrudes from the fuselage and the tail planes mount through a hole in the tail plane in-line with its main spar. This spigot acts as a pivot point with bearings inside the tail plane to allow it to easily rotate.

Each tail plane is held in place with a nut and locking washer. Towards the forward edge of each tail plane is the input arm which is the connection point for the hydraulic actuator (powered flying control unit or PFCU) which extends and retracts to move the tail plane leading edge up and down as demanded by the pilot. The PFCUs are installed behind a rectangular-shaped access panel either side of the rear fuselage underneath and inline to the leading edge of the tail planes. Each input arms go through two slots in the rear fuselage skin. The all flying tail plane can control the aircraft in pitch attitude with both surfaces moving in unison or they can work independently to control the aircraft in roll. This type of technology was revolutionary in the 1950s but is now standard on modern fighters today. The Sepecat Jaguar uses an "all flying tail plane" and the Panavia Tornado uses "tailerons".

WK275 was delivered to Civil Aircraft Test Section (CATS) Boscombe Down on 26 July 1957. Before the war A&AEE were also responsible for providing the Certificate of Airworthiness (COA) for civilian aircraft. During the war there were four 'squadrons' within the test organisation, each given a letter and a test speciality. Squadron A tested fighters and trainers, B, bombers, C specialised in naval aviation and D in airborne warfare and helicopters. There were no civilian aircraft produced during the war but in preparation for this eventuality CATS was established as the civilian aircraft licence section and employed about thirty civilians in this RAF section. There were three test pilots, two navigators, two radio operators and the rest were made up of technicians and administrative personnel. When the Air Registration Board (ARB) took on the COA for civilian aircraft in 1950, A&AEE did not want to lose the reputation and depth of experience built up by CATS, which then became a specialist test service for aircraft falling out of the main squadron's remit. One of these was the testing of the all flying tail of the Swift.

The A&AEE aircraft record card for WK275. Delivered on 26 July 1957 with 86.50 hours. The last entry on 28 November 1958 shows a mere 56.50 hours were flown in sixteen months. (*Boscombe Down Aviation Collection*)

A rather poor image of WK275 parked in a quiet area of Radlett airfield on 3 January 1960. (*R. L. Ward via Tim Wood*)

While at Boscombe most of WK275's flights were an average duration of an hour with two flights of two hours. During January 1959 it suffered service problems with fuel leaks, hydraulic failures, and a broken fuel pump. Twice the engine was removed and then throughout February and March it remained on the ground awaiting allotment to a test routine.

During the 1960s Denis Kay ran Manchester Tankers Limited which dealt in used commercial equipment. One source for stock was the MoD disposal listing and he often purchased redundant military equipment, mainly aviation related and had over the years purchased many old aero engines and on occasion complete aircraft.

Inspired by recollections of Mike Lithgow's speed record, Denis bid on WK275, and purchased it for £350 on an 'as and where' basis. Essentially, he had to take it in the condition he found it, from wherever it was located. Fortunately he had his own transport and staff who would collect the items he purchased.

Before collection had been arranged Denis found himself in discussions with Percy Sheppard of Upper Hill, Leominster in Hereford. Denis and Percy agreed on a deal whereby the Swift would be delivered to Herefordshire and Denis would collect a very large-scale model of a GL88 gas-cooled nuclear reactor, made by the Atomic Energy Board in the early 1960s for an expo in Canada.

Roy Harrison, who Denis had engaged to move WK275, arrived at de Havilland's Hatfield airfield on a Thursday morning in 1968; his task was to dismantle and transport WK275 to Leominster.

The Swift was mounted on an elaborate scaffolding structure where it had reportedly been used for acoustic tests and the effects of jet engine noise. Once the tests were complete it became redundant.

Fortunately for Roy several trainee fitters were lent to him to assist with the dismantling. A small crane was used to lift off each wing and then the fuselage was lowered from the high test bed. It was laid on the trailer of the articulated lorry, with almost a third hanging over the tail end. The wings were placed on sand bags on their leading edges and rested against the fuselage, cushioned by bags filled with cotton offcuts. The load was roped down and Roy checked that the tail was the highest point of the load before he set off at 1900 hrs.

Travelling behind the load in his car Roy noticed the great deal of interest drawn to the old jet. He also watched with a great deal of apprehension when around Hemel Hempstead the load had to pass under a set of electric rail power lines. They were fitted with bells hanging down to warn of any impending collision, but the tail of the Swift passed safely under with three inches to spare.

Arriving late on the Friday night he was warmly greeted by the Sheppard family who provided him with a meal, a beer, and a bed for the night. The next morning Percy Sheppard and his sons were on hand with a crane to off load their Swift. They laid the fuselage and wings on the ground, and it was later assembled and placed on the three brick and concrete plinths.

The Sheppard Years

Percy Sheppard had history in the aviation industry. Born in 1912 he lived in Brockworth within one mile of the Gloster Aircraft Company (GAC). After leaving school he had a variety of jobs until he found employment at GAC in 1932. Being in an essential service he remained with GAC during the war and rose to foreman level working on Hurricanes and then other aircraft such as the Typhoon.

After the war, he started a company named Industrial Metal Manufacturers who made the then very popular metal kitchen units. Keeping his links with aviation the company reportedly made some interior fittings for the Bristol Brabazon. By 1951 Percy had had enough of city life and he decided to change careers and moved to the Red Lion Inn at Upper Hill, Leominster. He wanted an aircraft to restore, and then display outside the pub to attract clientele and to name the pub after. In 1963 he bought Supermarine Spitfire LF MkXVIe TD135 for £25 after it was put up for sale or scrap.

Manufactured at Castle Bromwich in 1945, the Spitfire was almost immediately posted as an instructional airframe, and then became the first Spitfire

MkXVI delivered to 604 Squadron, RAF Hendon, on 23 March 1945 where it was coded NG-U. It served there until 1951 when it was allocated to 346 (Tynemouth) Squadron, Air Training Corps (ATC). Sometime toward the end of 1960 or early 1961 it was sent to RAF Dishforth and dumped as scrap.

When Percy received the Spitfire it was in very poor condition. He placed it in the large shed behind the pub and began to re-create the missing parts. By this time he had also begun a military surplus sales outlet and had on hand various parts required to carry out repairs. He had a consignment of propellers, not Spitfire props but good enough to do the job. He had to build new engine cowlings and as there was no engine he had to build the frame on which to place the finished metal sheets. He fitted the propeller, with spinner and behind it was an electric motor. When it was positioned on stone plinths at the entrance to the pub car park there was a charity collection box below it and each time money was placed in the box the propeller would turn.

The Red Lion name was changed to The Spitfire and the pub was fitted with seats from an airliner and in 1967 Percy purchased over 100 built Airfix plastic aircraft models which hung from the ceiling and above the bar.

The army surplus business brought in a variety of vehicles and equipment and, being in the business, when Percy heard about the Swift and already having one Supermarine aircraft he decided it would be good to have two, one on each side of the property. The aircraft would become well known and attract people to the pub and his business. Fortunately, after his family had a look in the cockpit Percy closed and sealed the canopy. The Swift was mounted on three stone plinths and a sign writer painted 'Sheppards Surplus' along the fuselage.

Percy sadly was suffering from lung cancer and at the young age of fifty-six years he died in December 1968. Son Derick along with

TOP TO BOTTOM,
LEFT TO RIGHT

TD135 was displayed outside the Spitfire pub with its canopy, cowlings and propeller fashioned by Percy Sheppard from parts obtained by his military surplus business. *(Dave Welch)*;

The Spitfire pub sign on a cold winter's day. *(Sheppard Family Collection)*;

WK275 the morning after delivery about to be unloaded by one of the Sheppards' cranes. It is interesting to note the method of transport and strapping used in those days. *(Sheppard Family Collection)*;

Once the Swift was mounted on three stone plinths it served as a useful carport. In the background are the more modern cranes hired out by the Sheppards. *(Sheppard Family Collection)*;

Carefully chocked and supplied with the original pilot's ladder that allows two youngsters to examine the cockpit. *(Sheppard Family Collection)*;

Percy Sheppard shows his son Andy the cockpit of WK275 in 1968. *(Sheppard Family Collection)*

TOP, LEFT AND RIGHT
An aerial view of the Sheppard's business premises, a treasure trove of old vehicles. The Spitfire pub is the white building behind the Spitfire. (*Sheppard Family Collection*);
A 1974 view of WK275 at Sheppards Surplus. The family were often approached by people who had taken aerial photographs of their famous landmark. (*via Tim Wood*)

BOTTOM, LEFT AND RIGHT
The sign on the outside wall of the pub. It now resides in a garden. (*Sheppard Family Collection*);
WK275 in 2006 after thirty-eight years on display at Leominster, Herefordshire. (*Francis Wallace*)

his two sisters and brother then ran the business. The pub ran until 21 February 1975 when Derick and his wife closed it and concentrated on their outdoor supplies operation.

Around this time, a person interested in the Spitfire offered the family a replica Spitfire in return for TD135, which was to be donated to a UK aviation museum. The Spitfire was removed in 1975 but no replica appeared. In very short time Derick was advised that TD135 had been exported to the USA where it changed hands five times before it was returned to Europe and to Belgium in 2004. It is now with former Belgian air force Colonel Eric Vormezeele, awaiting restoration at Brasschaat, the base for 'The Vormezeele Air Force'.

The Swift stood alone for another thirty-seven years. Ironically it was often mistaken for a Spitfire. Often a car or maybe two would be parked underneath its shade-giving wings and on one occasion a school teacher reversed her school bus into the port wingtip, damaging it severely and opening the structure to corrosion. Apart from that the airframe was left unmolested, no parts were removed, and the cockpit was left as it was in 1968. It gathered birds and soil and moisture. The Sheppards were often approached to sell the aircraft, but the unpleasant experience with the Spitfire made them very wary. It was only when they were closing the outdoor business that they decided to sell.

A side view of WK275 in 2006 with the famous 'Sheppards Surplus' signwriting on either side of the roundel. *(Francis Wallace)*; The damaged aileron which resulted in water damage and corrosion. *(Francis Wallace)*; The front wheel firmly bolted and chained to a metal post embedded in the concrete. *(Francis Wallace)*; The port wingtip and aileron were damaged by a school bus many years before. *(Francis Wallace)*; Looking inside the nose wheel well everything is in place. *(Francis Wallace)*; Remarkably complete, the starboard wheel well. *(Francis Wallace)*

Restoration

It was the sunniest March in England and Wales since 1929, but early on the morning of Wednesday 14 March 2012, Chris Wilson and his team from Jet Art Aviation, found Leominster shrouded in fog. They had arrived at Sheppards Surplus store in the small Herefordshire town to remove an iconic and famous landmark.

WK275 had become famous across Great Britain, and as the classic aircraft industry grew it was for many years the subject of great speculation as to its fate. Typically, it was reported as 'full of holes' that it would 'crumble if moved', anyone stepping on it would 'probably go straight through the bottom' or 'it was a shame such a rare beast was rotting away'. It had huge rarity value, it had a following and was well known. Even the RAF had been known to use it as a way point on aerial navigational exercises.

One day its soon-to-be new owner arrived at Jet Art Aviation's Selby base and as he relates later he was looking for an ejection seat. When he talked to Chris later about WK275 he was advised that it would require a great deal of work and was in poor condition. Within a few weeks, Chris received a phone call and the owner announced that he had purchased WK275 and would like Chris Wilson and the Jet Art team to collect the airframe and begin restoration work. This was the reason why the Jet Art Aviation crew found themselves at the end of a three-hour road trip in foggy Herefordshire.

They began the day balanced on scaffolding removing the tail planes that had not been taken off since the aircraft had been built.

LEFT TO RIGHT
The sight that greeted the Jet Art Aviation team when they arrived to remove WK275 on 14 March 2012. (*Jet Art Aviation*);
Faded nose art that had been applied while at Sheppards. (*Jet Art Aviation*)

TOP TO BOTTOM
The crane had taken the strain in anticipation of the Swift being cut free from the metal poles embedded in the plinths. *(Jet Art Aviation)*;
Mounted onto the heavy-duty transport trestles, work then began on the removal of the wings. *(Jet Art Aviation)*;
WK275 arrives at the Jet Art Aviation premises in March 2012. *(Jet Art Aviation)*

There were no manuals, but there was severe corrosion and forty-seven years of muck. They also managed to remove the wing fillet panels to gain access to the wing bolts. This involved undoing hundreds of flat countersunk screws that had been exposed to all weathers, grime, and wear over the years.

On day two the transport lorry arrived with a low-bed trailer, with a crane mounted on the rear. The team began to prepare for the lift. Because of the birds' nests, soil with growing plants and other sundry debris inside the airframe, an educated guess was required to work out the centre of gravity.

The undercarriage had been secured to the plinths by welding the legs to upright steel rods embedded in the brick. It was not possible to make a trial lift. Cutting the steel supports without securing the aircraft from the crane was dangerous as it may have slipped off its stands so the team only had one shot to get this right.

Two boat slings were positioned to lift at strong points within the fuselage and a long red-painted spreader beam above kept them in place. The crane driver took up the slack and two of the welds on the undercarriage legs were cut. The driver was warned the third was about to go. It was held by a small piece of metal that could not be cut of fear of damaging the oleo leg, which snapped under the pressure of the crane and WK275 was in the air for the first time in nearly five decades. Perfectly balanced.

Slowly they swung the arm of the crane through 90 degrees and lowered the Swift onto the heavy-duty trestles. Kindly, Newark Air Museum had previously allowed Chris access to their Swift FR5, WK277, to scribe and make card templates of the belly so fuselage trestles of the correct profile could be manufactured in advance of the job.

Both wings now hung over the side of the low-bed and the hard slog began. The crew found the three lift points on the wings, made connectors and slung each in turn. Although WD40 penetrating oil had been used, the bolts would not budge even with heavy hammer blows intended to shock the corroded bolts free. Oxy Acetylene was used as a last resort to expand the front, rear and main spars to create a gap however small that would allow the nine corroded bolts to be drilled out. To help ease the pressure on the bolts the crane took the weight of the wingtip. It took a long time to free the wings and to lay them down on the trailer resting on the extended undercarriage; which were too corroded to retract.

Day two ended at 2115 hrs. The lorry drivers had exceeded their hours and had to sleep in their cab in the Sheppards' yard. The Jet Aviation team arrived home well after midnight elated at what had been achieved. An aircraft that many had said would never come apart had been successfully dismantled.

The next day the fuselage was unloaded and lowered onto the transport trestles that had been formed using an old Rolls-Royce Avon engine stand. It stood outside the restoration building and the wings were laid against the side of the building. Within a few days, the undercarriage legs were freed up and retracted into the wings where they stayed until August 2016.

Strip down

A familiar site to many RAF ground crew; the engine covers off the Swift. *(Jet Art Aviation)*.

Almost immediately a full survey was completed to determine the true condition of the airframe and the extent of the work required. This showed that the bulk of the major structure had fared very well despite standing outside, exposed to the elements for nearly fifty years. The survey revealed two stunning finds.

The first was that within the fuselage was a completely original Rolls-Royce Avon Mk114 engine and even more excitingly it was still fitted with the afterburning jet pipe, constructed of an expensive nimonic alloy, that were actively sought after for scrap and is the only known one existence.

Jet Art engineer, Naylan Moore, spent many days unscrewing the three engine panels on top of the fuselage. The problem was that the screws were an old British gauge 3/8th BSF thread, no longer made and the steel they were made of had reacted with the aluminium panels. A heat gun, special screwdriver, combined with a great deal of care and patience was required, as the brief was to preserve the fasteners at all costs. As it turned out a boxed complete set of new screws were found in Halifax and on reassembly these were greased and the panels reattached.

When exposed the engine was in remarkably good condition, considering its time outside. It was covered in debris, the rubbers and pipes were perished, there

was evidence of corrosion and it was clear it would never run again.
An indication of the level of care and attention that went into the
restoration, is that Chris Wilson borrowed a Rolls-Royce Avon lifting
frame to be able to attain the right angle to be able to extract and lift
the engine in the way it would have been when in service. With no
manuals and guided by years of experience on jet-powered aircraft,
Chris and his team gently extracted and then placed the engine on
an Avon engine stand on 5 November 2012. The days spent on the
engine and jet pipe allowed the team to gain access to critical areas
of the airframe and carry out necessary treatment and preservation
of the long-neglected engine bay and internal rear fuselage.

The second find transported the Jet Art team into a remarkable
time capsule. Apart from simple curiosity to have a look inside, the
restoration required the replacement of all cockpit glazing, which
over the years had become UV damaged and opaque. The canopy
had been sealed probably around 1968 to protect it from water
ingress and in addition the runners had seized onto the rails.
Following much pushing, shoving and lubrication access was gained
by forcing the canopy jettison mechanism and the canopy was lifted
off to reveal a complete cockpit with the original 1950s instrumen-
tation, stick, throttle and ejection seat all still installed.

It was dirty and dusty and the birds had managed to find their
way in but fortunately did little damage. The cockpit was cleaned
and vacuumed and with exception to the seat being replaced as it
was severely perished and sun bleached. The rest of the interior was
left as found, down to the handwritten notations on the instrument
panel. WK275's owner had purchased a rare and complete Swift
simulator which donated its seat to the restoration.

Fuselage

With the engine and jet pipe removed it became clear that a
well-established ecosystem had established itself in the old aircraft.
There was over two inches of soil throughout the inside of the
fuselage. This had been blown in or been deposited by birds and
along with bird dropping, rotting vegetation and general debris,
small plants had thrived. To ensure WK275's long-term survival
one of the Jet Art team spent two weeks and many dustbin loads
removing all this detritus.

ABOVE
Paint remover was applied in
stages to the fuselage and wings
and then elbow grease applied to
clean the surfaces and prepare
them for a new coat of paint.
(Jet Art Aviation)

Once cleaned internally, a complete bare metal paint strip down
was begun on 1 June 2012. This entailed covering sections of the
aircraft in garish, gloopy pink chemicals and then a great deal of
rubbing to clean the surfaces. This clearly exposed the panels that had
been damaged and that required replacement or repair. The stripped
fuselage was mounted on a wheeled trolley and on 16 October 2012 it
was wheeled undercover.

An examination of the fuselage interior was undertaken and
essential anti-corrosion measures were adopted to prevent any
further deterioration and then repairs began on the exterior skin
and panels. The decision was taken to replace all panel fasteners,
even if the panel itself did not require any attention. The thinking
being that in the future having well prepared and easily removable
panels would facilitate on-going maintenance and anti-corrosion
measures. There were thousands of 2BA fasteners required as well
as accompanying anchor nuts.

Numerous areas of the belly of WK275 had suffered severe harm,
some from actual damage and ruptures and others from water
damage and the damp environment created by the soil, plants, and
bird life. Areas of the skin that were damaged were removed or cut

away. It was important to remove as small a section as possible, taking into consideration the underlying structure. Missing and damaged panels and frames were all replaced or repaired with the correct aviation grade aluminium, of the correct gauge, with holes drilled to original specifications. Where necessary additional underpinning sections were constructed and the new panels attached. Where it was possible to access both sides of a repair solid rivets were used, where not countersunk pop rivets came into play.

All the access panel fasteners were original steel items which were corroded. Finding the necessary old-style British standard components was incredibly difficult and near impossible to source from one supplier in the bulk required. Several small quantity purchases were made from wherever and whenever they became available in order to make up the numbers necessary to finish the project. Items such as countersunk screws used to secure most of the panels and anchor nuts, all needed sourcing and replacing in large quantities. This sheet metal work cannot really be seen on the restored airframe, but without remedial work it would have made a poor exhibit and the rot would have eventually consumed all that remained.

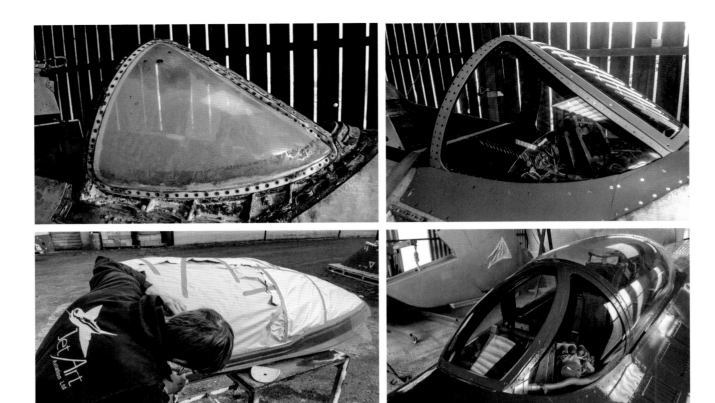

All the coaming had to be removed by the careful unscrewing of very reluctant fastenings and the area treated for corrosion. *(Jet Art Aviation)*;

Once the structure had been treated, new glazing was installed and the refurbished coaming replaced with all new screws. *(Jet Art Aviation)*;

A canopy in good condition from a simulator that Tim Wood had purchased was prepared and sprayed. *(Jet Art Aviation)*;

The refurbished cockpit with new glazing and a replacement seat from the simulator. The instruments were left as they were found. *(Jet Art Aviation)*

The canopy, side panels and front screen were all milky and had to be replaced. The simulator again stepped in and provided an almost pristine replacement main canopy, but the work around the forward screen frames was far more complex. There were hundreds of corroded steel screws that had to be carefully extracted from the magnesium alloy frame and only three had to be drilled out. The frames were fully treated and refurbished and new blown Perspex screens inserted. Work was also carried out on the wing roots. These were cleaned up, debris removed from the spar, corrosion treatment applied and the anchor nuts were replaced.

Somewhere in WK275's post-service life the top of the fin had been damaged and water and corrosion had taken hold. It required some complex metal work to restore the exact shape and integrity required for a proper restoration. A local Selby craftsman, 'Mick the Metal Magician', whose main business is the manufacture of motorbike fuel tanks cleverly recreated the form and shape which can be seen on the finished airframe.

Preparation for painting was completed with a final degrease. An undercoat etch primer was then applied and the correct colour code grey and green camouflage gloss top coat was applied to finish off

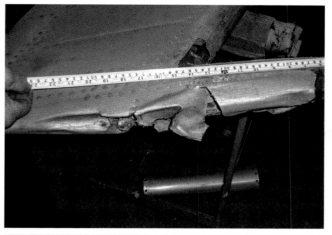

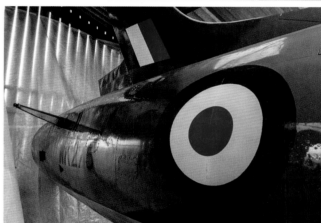

the upper surfaces. This comprising of dark sea grey and dark green upper surfaces with silver top coat applied to the lower surfaces with large black serial number applied on the underside of the wings. Markings, stencilling and RAF roundels/fin flash were the final finishing touches. Spray-through stencils were made and cut using the Swift at Tangmere museum as a guide for font sizes and location as well as studying photos of the aircraft when last in service. The brief was to make the external paint finish as accurate as possible to when last operated and flown, even down to retaining the red nose cone. Vintage 1960s photographs of the aircraft played a very important part in this process. Once all the painting was completed, dry clear plastic sheets were draped over the restored fuselage to protect it until final assembly.

Wings

The nature of the project was that time was put into the restoration in between the other work that Jet Art Aviation had on its schedule. This meant that work on the wings was mostly left until a definite home had been found and it was clear the aircraft could be assembled and remain undercover in a protective environment.

When working on the wings the most effective position was to have them resting on the leading edge or suspended in a similar position. This permitted work to be carried out on both sides and good access to open panels and the main undercarriage.

The port wing had been badly damaged by a truck at the Sheppards. This, like the tailfin underwent expert repair and to finish it off the red lens was shaped from that of a Panavia Tornado, cut to size and extensively reworked. Behind the lens a new bulb

LEFT TO RIGHT
Along with the damage to the wingtip, the port navigation lens had been destroyed. *(Jet Art Aviation);*
After the metal work repairs were complete. *(Jet Art Aviation);*
A lens was fashioned from one taken from a Panavia Tornado. The light bulb that was missing has been replaced. *(Jet Art Aviation)*

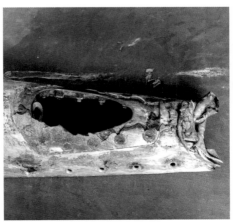

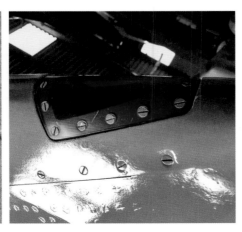

TOP TO BOTTOM,
LEFT TO RIGHT
As it arrived at Jet Art Aviation, the damaged port wing. *(Jet Art Aviation)*; On a trolley after strip-down and cleaning. The aileron had been sent for repair. *(Jet Art Aviation)*; Markings being applied to the underside of the completed wing. *(Jet Art Aviation)*; Ready to be reunited with the fuselage. *(Jet Art Aviation)*

was fitted to complete the repair. Both the ailerons required repair. The hinge pins were seized and the skills of Mick were again employed to return them to a workable condition. As there is no hydraulic pressure the ailerons are retained in position using English Electric Canberra locks. The flaps were opened, cleaned, treated for corrosion, and then prepped, primed and painted.

Repairs

The undercarriage legs, wheels and tyres were in very poor condition. The main wheels were sent away for repair and new tyres were sourced from a buyer on eBay. All three undercarriage oleos were stripped of the hand-painted blue colour, repaired and painted original silver, by Jet Art Aviation staff. The nose wheel itself fell apart with corrosion and fortuitously it was found that it was the same as a Hunter wheel which was easily sourced and fitted.

In a final push in August 2016 the wings were painted, the nose gear refitted and gags were made for the main undercarriage. These were required to prevent undercarriage sagging and were necessary because the age and lack of maintenance of the oleo struts made them unsafe to charge them with high pressure nitrogen.

Painted in its last 'as flown' service colour scheme of grey and green camouflaged upper surfaces and silver undersides, the finishing touches were made. As it never served in any squadron, this meant simply applying the standard 1960s roundels and fin flash and installing the jet pipe ready for final assembly at Doncaster.

Assembly

On Monday 21 November 2016, the wings were placed in custom-made frames and then loaded onto Second World War bomb trollies, strapped-down and craned onto a low-bed articulated trailer. On the Tuesday, they made the trip to Doncaster with a six-man crew, who then returned to Selby to load the fuselage. This was mounted on the same supporting frames that had been used four years before at Leominster. The wings and the fuselage had been prepared for final assembly with the landing wheels extended and fixed.

Assembly began on the Wednesday and took five men fifteen hours to carefully re-attach the wings to WK275 still mounted on the transporting trailer. They then pushed the almost complete aircraft undercover.

Thursday saw the process completed. The tail plane was fitted and the wing fillets fastened in place with 300 screws per side. The old-fashioned 2BA countersunk screws were almost impossible to find but an industrial shop in Halifax had a brand-new box with the exact number required. Then for the first time in nearly fifty years WK275 was attached to a tow bar and towed into her new hangar. She joined two other famous fellow Cold War warriors, Vulcan XH558 and English Electric Canberra WK163, of the Vulcan to the Sky Trust at Robin Hood Airport.

To reduce stresses on the airframe it was decided not to re-install the engine and it was cleaned up and mounted on an original Rolls-Royce Avon engine stand that had been found near Portsmouth at a marine salvage company and fortunately it had all the right connections.

Refurbishing WK275 involved a great deal more than simply a refresh. It was essential that to preserve this historical jet for the future a far more extensive undertaking was required than first envisaged. The preservation of WK275 will be an ongoing process that will see the aircraft preserved for future generations. An important piece of British Jet Age heritage has been saved and preserved.

Jet Art Aviation

Based in Yorkshire, Jet Art Aviation specialise in the supply of ex-military aircraft, museum aircraft, aircraft engines, cockpit sections, ejection seats, aircraft spares and collectibles. They are a specialist disposal contractor for aircraft/aircraft parts, undertake aircraft/component restoration work, aircraft engineering, aircraft transportation and logistical work to individual customer requirements. Providing a unique service offering a combination of items and services which cannot be found elsewhere.

By trade an engineering technician (airframe), Chris Wilson served for eight years in the RAF with two years as ground crew on the Red Arrows as an airframe mechanic working on both first and second line maintenance. A fantastic posting that was accompanied with plenty of travel as well as the opportunity to fly in the back seat of the Hawk jets.

After qualification as an airframe fitter, he served a tour on Tornado F3 aircraft with 11 Squadron at RAF Leeming. 11 Squadron again offered the opportunity of travel with exercises in Alaska, Florida, Oman and a stint in Saudi for Op Resinate South. Chris left the RAF to get married, settle down and run his own business in 2004, which he runs with his wife Mel. Their vision was originally to build bespoke aviation-themed furniture and display items.

Their business quickly evolved and over the next few years, market requirements changed the range of services and products on offer. The demand for fully documented aircraft parts and larger projects such as the restoration and the supply of complete aircraft for display use led to expanding the business. Jet Art Aviation developed into a small but skilled and highly professional limited company meeting customer needs throughout the UK and globally.

Servicing customers from commercial aircraft operators, large aviation museums, and the top end aviation collectors, Jet Art also support the enthusiast, smaller collector, while thousands of items supplied have been used on aircraft and cockpit restoration projects helping to preserve aviation history for generations to come. Aviation inspired furniture and display items are still produced and are regularly on display at art exhibitions.

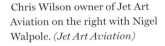

Chris Wilson owner of Jet Art Aviation on the right with Nigel Walpole. *(Jet Art Aviation)*

A series of then and now images of the restoration of WK275.
All images are by Jet Art Aviation, apart from the image on page 146
which was taken by Francis Wallace.

WK875 IN 2006 BEFORE RESTORATION

Owner's interest

My QUEST DURING THE Christmas period of 2011 was to purchase an ejection seat for my son Callum in order that he could play his computer games sat in a seat that could possibly have gone to war protecting our great nation. Jet Art in Selby had confirmed an initial meeting to look at their seats but to my surprise they also sold jet cockpits and complete aircraft.

After leaving their business I decided to trawl the internet and so came across Sheppards Surplus based in Leominster selling the only Supermarine Swift F4 fighter in the world. A meeting was convened at their Upper Hill site where I met Andrew Sheppard who told me all about the jet and how his grandfather Percy Sheppard had moved it back in 1968 from Hadfield to Upper Hill on the back of a truck for display purposes and to complement the Spitfire from the Second World War and other military vehicles there already.

A figure was agreed and agreement signed by all parties; for the next two months visits were made to help with the move. Jet Art was once again contacted to ask if they would be interested in lifting the jet and taking it up

Sandy Burns, Nigel Walpole, Tim Wood, Eric Sharp and Ian Waller at the Cold War Fast Jet Pilot Reunion at Old Warden in 2013. (*Tim Wood*)

LEFT TO RIGHT
A summary of the aircraft flown by
Peter Thorne while with A
Squadron of A&AEE shows the
tremendous skill and knowledge
Boscombe Down pilots had to
possess. *(Air Cdre Peter Thorne)*;
Supermarine Swift F4 WK275
alongside Hawker Hurricane GR3
XZ130 – pioneers from different
eras. *(Jet Art Aviation)*

to Selby for a refresh and paint, this was agreed and the move took
place in March 2012.

Wind the clock forward four-and-a-half years and F4 WK275
has been completed and put on display with Vulcan XH558 at
Doncaster Sheffield Airport for all to see and marvel at its beautiful
lines and authentic transformation. During the four-and-a-half
years the simulator for the Swifts was also purchased and this then
allows the full story to be told from pilot training to flying this
amazing aircraft. In addition, we were also able to source original
APs (Air Publications) of the airframe and the Rolls-Royce Avon
engine maintenance manuals.

It is pleasing to note that WK275 is complete and after speaking
to the first pilot Air Commodore Peter Thorne (2015) he confirmed
that F4 WK275 was in his top 10 of 100 aircraft that he test flew
over an illustrious flying career.

When you think of all the modern jets both military and commercial, much is owed to the pilots, technical staff and designers of
the early jets such as the Swift. Aspects such as engine noise and
vibration testing, variable incidence tail wings and slab rudder to
aid stability, powered controls and safety were all required when
flying at speeds approaching 730 mph.

I would therefore like to acknowledge publicly the amazing work
of the Jet Art Aviation team who helped make this all possible.

Tim Wood

Specifications and marks

SWIFT F4 AIRCRAFT DATA	
Aircraft Type	Swift F4
First Flight	27 May 1953
Engine	Rolls-Royce Avon RA7R axial flow jet engine
Maximum Thrust	7,500 lb (cold) 9,450 lb (with reheat)
Range	793 km / 493 miles
Loaded Weight	8,965 kg / 19,764 lb
Max Speed (at sea level)	1,141km/h / 709 mph
Initial Rate of Climb	4,432 m/min / 14.450 ft/min
Service Ceiling	11,887 m / 39,000 ft
Time to 12,192 m/ 40,000 ft	5.7 min (clean and reheat) 6.5 min (belly tank and reheat)
Armament	Four 30-mm Aden cannons
Wing Span	32 ft 4 in
Length	41 ft 5.5 in
Height	13 ft 6 in

Type	Mark	Engine	Prod	Comments
510		Rolls-Royce Nene	1	Attacker with swept-flying surfaces and tail wheel
517		Rolls-Royce Nene	1	All moving rear fuselage
535		Rolls-Royce Nene	1	Nose wheel
541		Rolls-Royce R AJ65 Avon	2	Avon prototypes
541	F1	Avon RA-7/108	20	No afterburner, two Aden cannons
541	F2	Avon RA-7/109	16	No afterburner, four Aden cannons, wing fences
541	F3	Avon RA-7A/114	25	With afterburner, two Aden cannons
546	F4	Avon RA-7A/114	8	Variable incidence tail plane, afterburner, four Aden cannons
549	FR5	Avon RA-7A/114	98	Lengthened nose with three cameras, frameless canopy, afterburner, two Aden Cannons
552	F7	Avon RA-7A/116	14	Lengthened nose for radar, four Aden cannons and four Fairey Fireflash air-to-air missiles

Absolute speed records 1953 and Royal Flush competitions

	ABSOLUTE SPEED RECORDS 1953			
Date	**Pilot**	**Aircraft**	**Speed**	**Place**
16 July 1953	Lt Col William Barns	North American F-86D Sabre	715.6 mph	Salton Sea, California
7 Sept 1953	Neville Duke	Hawker Hunter Mk3	727.6 mph	Littlehampton, UK
25 Sept 1953	Mike Lithgow	Supermarine Swift F4	737.5 mph	Castel Idris, Tripoli, Libya
3 October 1953	James Verdin USN	Douglas XF4D-1 Skyray	752.7 mph	Salton Sea, California
29 October 1953	Frank Everest USAF	North American F-100 Super Sabre	755.1 mph	Salton Sea, California

Note: The Swift was a production model fitted with an RA7 Avon with afterburner and its normal four-cannon armament. The Hunter, also powered by an RA7 Avon, was a prototype, with a tapered nose and no armament.

ROYAL FLUSH COMPETITIONS

Year	Royal Flush	Base	Country
1956	I	held at French AF Base Lahr	West Germany
1957	II	held at RAF Base Laarbruch	West Germany
1958	III	held at USAF Base Spangdahlem	West Germany
1959	IV	held at KLu Base Eindhoven	The Netherlands
1960	V	held at French AF Base Bremgarten	West Germany
1961	VI	held at Belgian AF Base Beauvechain	Belgium
1962	VII	held at USAF Base Ramstein	West Germany
1963	VIII	held at RAF Base Wildenrath	West Germany
1964	IX	ending at USAF Base Alconbury	United Kingdom
1965	X	ending at German AF Base Fürstenfeldbruck	West Germany
1966	XI	ending at French AF Base Strasbourg	France
1967	XII	ending at KLu Base Twenthe	The Netherlands
1968	XIII	ending at Canadian AF Base Lahr	West Germany
1969	XIV	ending at RAF Base Brüggen	West Germany
1970	XV	held at KLu Base Deelen	The Netherlands
1971	XVI	held at USAF Base Ramstein	West Germany
1973	XVII	held at Belgian AF Base Florennes	The Netherlands
1975	XVIII	held at French AF Base Bremgarten	West Germany

Operators and survivors

OPERATORS	
Mark	**Operator**
F1	56 Squadron RAF
F2	56 Squadron RAF
F3	Nil
F4	C Squadron A&AEE
FR5	II (AC) Squadron RAF, 4 Squadron RAF, 79 Squadron RAF
F7	No. 1 Guided Weapons Development Squadron

SURVIVORS	
Serial	**Location**
VV106	Type 517 stored by the Fleet Air Arm Museum, Yeovilton
WK198	Fuselage only at Brooklands Museum, Surrey
WK275	On loan to the Vulcan To The Sky Trust
WJ277	On display at the Newark Air Museum
WK281	On display at the Tangmere Military Aviation Museum
XF113	Cockpit only Boscombe Down Aviation Collection
XF114	G-SWIF is stored by Solent Sky, Southampton

Bibliography

ANDREWS, C.F. & MORGAN, E. B., *Supermarine Aircraft since 1914*, Putnam, 1989.

BIRTLES, P., *Postwar Military Aircraft 7, Supermarine Attacker Swift and Scimitar*, Ian Allan Ltd, 1992.

BOYNE, W. J., 'The Evolution of Jet Fighters: A New Point of View', *Air & Space Power Journal*, January-February 1984.

CHORLTON, M., *Supermarine, Company Profile 1913-1963*, Kelsey Publishing Group, 2012.

COLLIER-WEBB, D., 'Tested & Failed – Supermarine Swift', *Aeroplane*, Vol. 23, No. 8, Issue 292, August 1997.

COLLIER-WEBB, D., 'Tested & Failed – Supermarine Swift', *Aeroplane*, Vol. 23, No. 9, Issue 293, August 1997.

FLIGHT magazine, 25 June 1954.

FLIGHT magazine, 25 February 1955.

FREEMAN, SQUADRON LEADER A.F., 'The Post-War Auxiliary Air Force, Royal Air Force Reserve and Auxiliary Forces', *Royal Air Force Historical Society Journal*, 2003.

GOLLEY, J., *Jet: Frank Whittle and the Invention of the Jet Engine*, Datum Publishing Limited, 2010.

GORDON, D., *Tactical reconnaissance in the Cold War: 1945 to Korea, Cuba, Vietnam and The Iron Curtain*, Leo Cooper Ltd, 2007.

HC Deb, Vol. 458 cc839-41, 22 November 1948.

HC Deb, Vol. 494 cc371-2, 21 November 1951.

Hallion, Dr R. P., (Ed.), *NASA's Contributions to Aeronautics,* National Aeronautics and Space Administration, 2010.

Hansard, Vol. 197 cc 474-99, 16 May 1956.

Hansard, Vol. 503, 16 July 1952.

Hansard, Vol. 508 cc 1775-82, 4 December 1952.

Hansard, Vol. 537 cc 2066-199, 2 March 1955.

Hutchinson, K., 'SYLT Part 2', *First & Last, the Journal of the Halton 81st Entry,* Issue 39, May 2014.

Jones, G., *The Jet Pioneers – The Birth of Jet-Powered Flight,* Methuen, 1989.

Lake, J., 'Vickers Supermarine Swift', *International Air Power Review,* Vol. 19, Airtime Publishing, 2006.

Lockley, E. M., *Into the Jet Age: Chilbolton Airfield 1945- 1962,* Holmes & Sons, 1999.

Loftin L. K., *Quest for Performance : The Evolution of Modern Aircraft,* NASA Special Publication, 1985.

Lorell, M. & Levaux H. P., *The Cutting Edge: A Half Century of US Fighter Aircraft R&D,* RAND Corporation, 1998.

McDevitt, J. B., 'An Experimental Investigation of Two Methods for Reducing Transonic Drag of Swept-Wing and Body Combinations', National Advisory Committee for Aeronautics, Washington, 1955.

Macfadyen, Air Marshal I., 'Defensive Operations, Royal Air Force in Germany 1945-1993', Royal Air Force Historical Society Seminar, 9 December 1998.

Onderwater, H., *Second to None, The History of No. II (AC) Squadron Royal Air Force 1912-1992,* Airlife Publishing, 1992.

Pitchfork, Air Commodore G. R., 'Reconnaissance, Royal Air Force in Germany 1945-1993', Royal Air Force Historical Society Seminar, 9 December 1998.

Quinault, R., 'Britain 1950', *History Today,* Vol. 51, Issue 4, April 2001.

Rolls-Royce, *The Jet Engine*, The Technical Publications Department, Rolls-Royce plc, 1996.

Roussel, M., *Spitfire's Forgotten Designer, The Career of Supermarine's Joe Smith*, The History Press, 2013.

Segel G., *The Defence Industrial Base and Foreign Policy*, Glen Segel, London, 31 January 1998.

Thorne, P., Oral History Recordings, Imperial War Museum, http://www.iwm.org.uk/

Walpole, N., *Swift Justice: The Supermarine Low-Level Reconnaissance Fighter (2nd ed.)*, Pen & Sword Books, 2004.

Waterton, W. A., *The Quick and the Dead*, Grub Street Publishing, 2012.

Williams, A. G., 'The Development of RAF Guns and Ammunition from World War I to the Present Day', *Royal Air Force Historical Society Journal 45*, 2009.

Winn, Group Captain C. V., Operations Record Book, Royal Air Force Laarbruch, Laarbruch F540 1957– May, Royal Air Force Museum Laarbruch – Weeze.e.V.

http://www.56sqnfirebirds.org.uk/index.htm

http://www.81st-entry.co.uk/journals/articles/journal-39-article5.html

http://archive.aviationweek.com/

http://www.belgian-wings.be

http://www.flightglobal.com/pdfarchive

http://www.kle.nw.schule.de/laarbruch-museum/html/ENG/index_ENG.htm

http://www.milaviation.com/

http://www.millionmonkeytheater.com/Swift.html

http://www.thunder-and-lightnings.co.uk/

http://www.ventnorradar.co.uk/

Index